You Can't Go Wrong Trusting God: A Collection of True Stories

Nick Nichols

Published by Nick Nichols, 2023.

YOU CAN'T GO WRONG TRUSTING GOD: A COLLECTION OF TRUE STORIES

First edition. May 24, 2023.

ISBN: 979-8223265160

Written by Nick Nichols.

Table of Contents

I dedicate this book to the Lord Jesus Christ who makes all things new!...and who made my life profoundly new on February 2, 1971. Without Jesus, there would be absolutely no stories to tell.

~~~

"For God so loved the world that he gave his one and only Son, that whoever believes in him shall not perish but have eternal life." --John 3:16 (NIV)

~~~

I also dedicate this book to our adult children Holly, Heather, Christian, Brittany, and our three unborn children in heaven, Jonathan, Jessie, and Jordan.

~~~

Lastly, this book is dedicated to Barb, my lovely wife of forty-five years, without whom the reader would have a more difficult time understanding what I wrote. God knew best and married me to a live-in grammarian who rescued me from dangling participles, split infinitives, comma splices and the dreaded squinting modifiers!
~~~

Do Angels Drive Mercedes?

<<>>

Sitting in my car in the trashy alley by the river in Pittsburgh, I was completely lost. I had driven through so much new construction that my map was worthless. The waning rays of day cast shadows through the large bridge I was sitting under making the area look even more hostile and not a place to be caught alone in the dark. Sighing, I thought, "I'll never make it to the seminar. At least not on time, and I hate being late!"

It started the week before when I heard about a seminar on the struggling church in China being held at a church in Pittsburgh, Pennsylvania. Everything seemed to be at the last minute: discovering the seminar, calling the last day of enrolment and getting permission to leave work early on short notice. But the Lord had placed China in my heart, and I really wanted to attend that seminar. Time wise, getting there was going to be tight since I was driving from Columbus, Ohio.

Now there I sat at 6:45 p.m. with the seminar starting in fifteen minutes. I prayed, "Lord, I am lost, and I really don't want to be late. Please help me to find my way to the church. In the name of Jesus, Amen." Just then a Mercedes pulled out of a side street right in front of me, and I had this sudden strong urge to follow the car. It turned left out of the alley, and I turned left following. We went down the road, turned right, cut through another alley, turning left onto the main road. We passed through a four-way stop, turned right and followed a short detour of orange signs. We made more turns through some construction and came to a traffic light turning yellow.

We slowed to a stop, but just before the light turned red, the Mercedes took off straight through the intersection leaving me stuck at the red light. As I watched it disappear into the traffic, I looked at my watch . . . Three minutes to go. I thought, "Have I been stupid?" The light turned green, and as I was passing through the intersection, I noticed a church on my right. It was THE church with the entrance to the parking lot right in front of me! I parked, went in, sat down, looked at my watch, one minute till seven! The speaker stood up and said, "Let's get started."

To be honest, I didn't hear the first few minutes of his talk. I was sitting there marveling at what had transpired in the last fifteen minutes. I wondered, "Do angels drive Mercedes?" Then my mind passed from that thought to a Scripture I had read long ago. In Psalms 22:5 it says, *"They called to You and escaped from danger; they trusted You and were not disappointed."* (GNT)

I trusted, and I was not disappointed.

You can't go wrong trusting God!

~~ **The End** ~~

The Hitchhiker and Two Eggs

<<>>

The only food we had was a dozen eggs. The hungry hitchhiker ate ten of the eggs, leaving us with two. That left my wife and me with one egg each. Earlier that week on Thursday evening, we'd received a call from a friend who lived several hours away saying she and her husband were having some terrible marriage problems! She wanted to know if we could come down and spend time talking with them.

My wife and I had just returned from living in Canada, purchased our first mobile home, I had enrolled in our local state university, and my wife had gotten a job all in our first week back from Canada. All that activity left us with zero dollars!! So when our friend called, we wanted to help but had no money for gas to go see them. I prayed, "Lord, if you want us to go help them, then you'll need to provide some money for gas."

Friday, the next day, to my surprise I received a check in the mail for ten dollars from the IRS. It had been sent to my previous New York college address; they eventually forwarded it to my parents, who sent it to my college address in Canada, where it got lost by the school, and didn't get found until I was long gone from Canada, and I received it at our new address eight months later! The money was late, but right on time to go help our friends! Back then, ten dollars bought enough gas to drive down to our friends and back with no problem.

With a tank full of gas, we drove down that evening, spending the night with our friends and discussing their problem. We spent Friday evening and most of Saturday listening and praying with them and then on Saturday evening we said our goodbyes. On our way back to our home, we picked up three hitchhikers since, in our old Ford van, we had plenty of room. Later, I saw another hitchhiker and told him to jump in as well. After an hour, the first three had gotten to where they wanted to go, so I dropped them off on the side of the road, leaving us with the lone hitchhiker.

In answer to the question of where the hitchhiker was planning to go, he said, "I'm headed out West and thought I would find a place to sleep in the weeds off the road on the west side of town." I told him we lived on the west side of town, and he could stay overnight with us, and then in the morning on my way to school, I could drop him off at the highway. He said, "That sounds great to me if you don't mind, and it sure beats the weeds!!" As we drove in the dark, we shared with him about the Lord and His work in our lives and how Jesus had set us free and given us peace in our hearts. We got home very late, and we all went straight to bed—his bed being a weed-free couch in our little living room.

My wife left early in the morning for work. When the hitchhiker and I got moving, I asked him if he'd like some eggs for breakfast. (Since that was the only food we had!) "Sounds GREAT!" he said. He was a hungry dude and ate ten of our twelve eggs, unknowingly leaving my wife and me with two eggs to share for a later meal. Our current food supply had been a continual urgent matter of prayer. We would continue to trust the Lord for our food even though we only had two eggs. I started thinking of ways to enjoy our last two eggs. I was thinking about hard boiling them, cutting them in half and laying the two halves yolk-side down on each plate. On the one half, I was going to push in a birthday-type candle and on the second half paint a smiley face with food coloring. I planned on surrounding them with wildflowers from out back by the railroad tracks behind our mobile home and enjoy our two remaining eggs by candlelight.

Later that day, my wife came home all excited saying, "I got my first check!! I got my first check!!" We went to the grocery store and had a nice supper. But part of me thought that the university where she was now working would have held back her first two weeks' of pay and so she wouldn't be paid till the end of her fourth week. No matter, we were happy to have the money and some food to eat. While eating, though, she said, "I think they made a mistake on my check and overpaid me."

The next day she went in and spoke with the payroll department about her check error. The lady there said, "There is no error on the check, but HOW IN THE WORLD DID YOU GET YOUR CHECK??" She continued, "You're a new instructor, and we hold back your first two weeks' of pay. I'll have to look into this." Turns out, that my wife's check had somehow accidentally gotten mixed up with the janitor's checks and was handed out to her two weeks ahead of time! When we had no money and only two eggs, the Lord blessed us with an early payday . . . Knowing our needs and going before us to provide exactly what we needed exactly when we needed it!

"So don't worry about these things, saying, 'What will we eat? What will we drink? What will we wear?' These things dominate the thoughts of unbelievers, but your heavenly Father already knows all your needs. Seek

the Kingdom of God above all else, and live righteously, and he will give you everything you need." —Matthew 6:31-33 (NLT)

~~ The End ~~

One Attack Dog, One Prayer, One Harmonica

<<>>

Cutting through a wooded alley on the way home from high school, I saw a German Shepard about fifty feet away. He was half grown and was watching me. I love critters of all kinds—dogs, cats, raccoons, snakes—you name it, and I liked them. Not being sure if the dog was friendly, I thought I would use the nice guy approach, so stooping a bit and patting my knees, I said, "Come here boy!!" He put his head down and came straight to me.

As I reached out to pet him, he suddenly growled and grabbed my leg just above the knee. He didn't just bite and run like most dogs; he stayed there gnawing on my leg. By the time I beat him off, he had torn my pants, and I was pretty bloody! I had been chewed on before by a lot of animals trying to catch them for fun, but this time it was pretty painful. I remember thinking that I was glad he wasn't a full-grown adult, or things could have been much worse!

Now fast forward about twenty years later, and my wife and I and three little kids are in the early stages of our three-month, three-country, and 15,100-mile road trip in an old VW camper van. During that trip, one of the things we enjoyed was showing up on the steps of old friends and surprising them. On this stop, we were around Albany, New York, and were stopping in to see the parents of a college friend.

We pulled onto their property, parking under an ancient old tree for shade. Their place used to be part of a large farm but now consisted of only a house and barn. Not seeing any other cars around, I told my wife I would go and see if anyone was home. Jumping out of the van, I walked over to the back door and knocked. That's when I heard a familiar sound, the growling of a German Shepard! He was a full-grown adult about a hundred feet away. He looked and acted like a trained attack dog! I pounded on the door more, and he put his ears back and started growling, barking, baring his teeth, and moving in closer. Memories flooded my mind of being attacked in the alley as a kid.

I looked back at the van and my wife and figured a plump guy like me couldn't run fast enough back to the van before he would get me. There was a lawn chair near me but fighting him off with that while trying to get back to the van didn't seem promising. And there was nothing near me to climb up. I had the keys, so my wife couldn't drive the van to me. I started praying, "Lord, I'm in trouble, please help me in Jesus name, Amen!!"

As soon as I said, "Amen," this thought from the Holy Spirit entered my mind, "Quick, take the harmonica out of your shirt pocket and play it!" The attack dog started moving in; I jammed the harmonica in my mouth and started banging out a loud rendition of, "When the Roll is Called up Yonder." The Shepard stopped, dropped his ears, turned, and sauntered back into the barn. I didn't know if someone in the family there played the harmonica, and he thought I was that person or that my playing was so bad he couldn't take it and went back into the barn!

Either way, I played my harmonica all the way back to the van, jumped in, and shouted, "Thank you, Jesus!!" And I meant it with all my heart! Later, I spoke with our college friend about stopping by to see her parents.

The first thing she asked was, "How did you get past the retired police dog!?" I chuckled, told her the story, and while she shook her head in amazement, I once again thanked Jesus for rescuing me!

"Trust in the LORD with all your heart, and lean not on your own understanding; in all your ways acknowledge Him, and He will make your paths straight." —Proverbs 3:5,6 (BSB)

~~ The End ~~

Toilet Paper from Heaven

<<>>

My wife stood in the store debating. Should she buy the white tissue paper she used for stuffing gift bag presents or not? With nearly all of our money now going to our twin daughter's college education, even little money decisions had become a big deal. She prayed about it and decided that she could get by without it for now. A few days later, she was going through a bag my uncle had given us of things he didn't want to take with him when he moved to Florida. In the bottom of the bag, she found two brand new, unopened packages of white tissue paper used for stuffing gift bag presents. She thought to herself, "God has provided again!"

While telling me about the tissue paper, my wife started to get real quiet, and with a smile and a tear in her eye, she said, "Remember the toilet paper prayer?" My mind thought back; how could I ever forget the toilet paper prayer. Many years ago I had a business go under, and I was forced against my will into bankruptcy. We lost everything except for some basic necessities and an old car. Life for our four children and us had become very difficult. But the Lord was faithful despite my business error and provided us with food, clothing, and a place to live while I was trying to find a job.

Incredibly, soon after, I received a job offer from my former boss who had employed me six years earlier, but I would have to start at an entry-level salary, which was about half of what I was making when I left the job. Now that we again had an income, and since we had lost our house, we needed to find a place that would rent to a family of six. My wife called more than 150 apartments in our large city and only found two apartments that we could afford that would accept a family of six. We rented a townhouse and moved in. The rent was high, and money was extremely tight. As we were adjusting to our new budget, there was one thing that constantly gnawed at my wife—just a little thing, and a little bit private.

She was bothered about how much toilet paper the six of us were using and the cost of buying it. So, one evening, not having a clue how in the world God could answer this, she prayed. "Lord, I know this is a little thing, but could you please provide us with a cheap source of toilet paper?"

Unbelievably, a short time later my father called and asked if we wanted some extra toilet paper! My wife couldn't believe her ears, and barely managed to say, "Of course!" The school where he was working as head custodian had decided to switch from using the little squares of toilet paper to the giant rolls that are now found in most public restrooms. He had to change all the toilet paper dispensers in the whole school. The administrator told him to get rid of the toilet paper squares.

He thought it would be a real shame to throw them in the recycling bin, so he decided to use them and give us a case of toilet paper whenever we needed one. Well, we used those squares for about four years! By the time he ran out of the cases at the school, my income had improved sufficiently that buying toilet paper was no longer an issue. My wife had prayed, and the Lord had provided! To us, it was indeed toilet paper from heaven!

"Casting all your care upon Him, for He cares for you." —I Peter 5:7 (KJV)

~~ The End ~~

Donuts and Auto Parts

<<>>

"May I help you," the young man said as he walked toward us with his elderly Grandmother in tow on his arm. Our VW Camper Bus was sitting in a small grocery store parking lot on the outskirts Bakersfield, California. The motor's generator had died, and our last battery jump had gotten us to this place. We had been standing beside the van praying about what to do next.

My wife and I with three toddlers had just driven 12,000 miles through the United States and Mexico with 3,000 miles to go through Canada back to home in Columbus, Ohio. The young man continued, "Do you need to have that thing fixed? If so, you're in luck, right around the corner is the best VW shop in town." After finishing the directions, the van barely started, and we limped our way around the corner to the repair shop.

The van had developed two problems during the trip, the generator dying and our master brake cylinder had started leaking pretty badly. I had to pour brake fluid in every time we stopped, and I was very concerned that we could lose our brakes in the mountains and not be able to stop.

It was Saturday, and the shop was only going to be open about three more hours. That should have been plenty of time to install a generator and rebuild a master brake cylinder. But there was a problem. Our VW Camper Van was nearly 20 years old, and they had a hard time locating a generator. Finally, they found the only parts shop in town that carried that old of a generator. They only had one left. That was the good news; the bad news was for our master brake cylinder, nobody in town had a new one, or a used one, or even a rebuild-it kit!

By this time it was an hour until the shop closed and we decided to take a walk and pray about the problem while they installed the generator. As my wife and I walked hand in hand, with our kids trailing, I prayed, "Dear Lord, I'm really worried about our brakes. If they would go out on the highway or in the mountains, we could be killed. Please solve this problem for us. In Jesus name, Amen."

About that time we were walking past a little donut shop. It looked like a house that someone had converted into a store. The kids were hungry, so we went in to buy some donuts and head back to the repair shop. While the kids were pointing and wanting every donut in the house, I noticed some old glass cases off to the side.

Out of curiosity, I walked over and looked into a dusty old case. Apparently, they used to sell auto parts as well as donuts! Then my eyes landed on something familiar. It looked like a gasket kit with the word VW in small print. The rest of the package was too dirty to read. I called the owner over, and she unlocked the case and handed it to me. I cleaned off the dirt, and it was a master brake cylinder rebuild-it kit for the exact same make, model and year as our van! I was amazed!

Heading back to the repair shop with our brake parts we were praising the Lord for hearing and answering our prayer.

We were all happy.

My wife and I were full of joy, and the kids were full of donuts.

"For my thoughts are not your thoughts, neither are your ways my ways," declares the Lord.

"You will go out in joy and be led forth in peace..." —Isaiah 55:8,12 (NIV)

~~ The End ~~

Parking-Pit in Mexico

<<>>

That evening I learned that God not only had parted the Red Sea, but He could also part a crowd of people. Nobody had been run over, and I was safe on the other side. I was so grateful to the Lord. But I didn't understand the shocked look on my wife's face!!

Our day had started in Mexico City. My wife and I learned about a small town southwest of the city called Taxco, which was famous for its silver artisans. Since we would be driving south to Oaxaca, with Taxco being somewhat on the way, we decided to stop and do some shopping.

After arriving in this quaint little village situated on the side of a mountain, we discovered Taxco was so crowded with tourists and locals that it was difficult to find a place to park. Eventually, we found a rather unusual location. It was a square pit about fifty feet deep with one single steep lane to get in and out of the parking-pit. Other cars were parked down there, so I cautiously drove our van down.

Our van was packed inside and loaded on top. My wife and I with our three kids were on a three-month road trip in a twenty-year-old VW camper van. We had so much luggage on top of the van that back in the States at Niagara Falls, I had managed to get our van sandwiched between the ceiling and floor in a parking garage. We couldn't budge until I unloaded some folding chairs off the top. Being so loaded had me pretty concerned about our brakes giving out as I drove us down the steep drive into the parking-pit.

After I got the van parked and secured, we went shopping. Taxco was a beautiful town with narrow, twisting cobblestone streets and homes with white stucco walls and red tiled roofs. The old colonial town's main plaza had multiple silver shops in any direction one looked. There were people everywhere, and the atmosphere was one of gala-enterprise. We had a great time! The locals were very friendly, and the silver work was excellent and cheap! We were enjoying ourselves so much that we stayed a little longer than we should have, and it was beginning to get dark.

Surprisingly, as dusk set in, the activity in the plaza increased. Even more people began to come out after dinner to enjoy the evening. It was so hard to leave, but we had business in Oaxaca the following day and had to go. We worked our way through the crowds in the plaza back to our van. While walking down the steep drive, I didn't say anything to my wife, but I began having doubts about our van being able to make it back up out of the parking-pit.

After paying the parking attendant, we all piled into the van, and I started the old engine. Sometimes it took a few tries, but this time the engine turned right over, coughed, belched some blue smoke and then we started up the steep drive. About a third of the way up, the strain was too much; the engine died, and we rolled backward down the drive to where I had started. This time I gave it more gas and hit the drive faster. That took us about two-thirds of the way up before the engine conked out. We again rolled back to start.

I had my wife and kids get out to lighten the load, then I revved up the engine and hit the steep drive going as fast as I could. The van sounded like it was going to blow. Just as I made it to the top of the drive, I slammed on my brakes; there were too many people in the way, and I knew I couldn't drive up onto the level street without hitting someone. Then the van died, and I rolled back down to where my family was standing.

Now, my wife was looking worried. Our three young children thought it was great fun watching their Poppy drive up and down, and up and down. I told my wife that she would have to go up on the street and stop the people at the top of the drive so I could get out without running over anybody. By this time it was dark, and the street lights threw an eerie cast of dancing shadows over us and the pit. Reluctantly, my wife said she would try to stop the crowd, and when it was clear, she would signal me with a wave of her hand.

I prayed, "Lord, somehow please help me get out of this pit without killing anyone." It was a simple prayer from the bottom of my heart; then up went my wife with the kids in tow. I sat at the bottom of the drive revving my engine and waiting. It seemed like it was taking her forever—then I saw it, her signal. I hit the gas. The engine was straining, but I was flying up that drive like a speeding bullet! With one big bump, I crested the drive and stopped right in the middle of the level street.

Praise the Lord! I hadn't run over anybody! My wife came running over with an awful look on her face and yelled, "Why did you come up!!?? I didn't signal you!!!" Stunned, I said in disbelief, "But I saw you signal me!" Then I noticed standing behind her was a large crowd of people about twenty feet from the van looking at us. I turned and looked out the opposite window and saw another large crowd of people about twenty feet from the van also staring at us. There was an empty zone, void of people on both sides of the van.

I suddenly realized the Lord had just performed a miracle!! For Moses, God had parted the waters; for us, He had parted the people! No one was hurt. I was profoundly amazed. My wife was relieved. And the kids wanted to see Poppy do it again!

"Then Moses stretched out his hand over the sea, and all that night the LORD drove the sea back with a strong east wind and turned it into dry land. The waters were divided, and the Israelites went through the sea on dry ground, with a wall of water on their right and on their left." —Exodus 14:21,22 (NIV)

PS: This is my wife's comment after editing this story: "Yep!!! Truly amazing to this very day!! Some things can ONLY be explained by God."

~~ The End ~~

Brakes & Grace

<<>>

"Poppy," my youngest daughter said, "my brakes make this terrible grinding sound when I step on them!" She was calling from her college in Nyack, New York, and I was in Columbus, Ohio. There wasn't much I could do but tell her to take her car to the nearest car repair shop as soon as possible. A bit later she called, "Poppy, I made it to the repair shop, but now I can't even get my car to move forward or backward . . . and neither can the repair guy!"

After looking at the brakes, the repair guy told me, "Your daughter is very, very, lucky this didn't happen while she was driving. The brake pad backing had somehow turned and dug into the caliper and rotor and jammed the wheel to keep it from turning. The wheel has mechanically frozen in place. Had that happened while she was driving, she could have had a very serious accident!"

Grateful the Lord had kept her safe brought back vivid memories of the Lord keeping me safe one time when my brakes went out at 55 mph! I was getting ready to head off for my second year of college and had been praying for a car. Not having much money as a college student, it needed to be cheap! One day my uncle stopped by and said he was buying a new car, and I could have his old one. Well, FREE trumps cheap! I said, "Thank you very much!!" Another Praise the Lord, and I had a car for college. Now, this was a long time ago, and the car was a 1963 Mercury Comet, a big heavy boat of a car with tail fins over the tail lights.

About a month after I got up to my college in Nyack, New York, located near the Hudson River, I noticed my front brakes making some noise. One morning I jacked my car up in the school parking lot and pulled off the wheel and drum to look at the drum brakes. (Cars didn't have disk brakes back then.) The two curved brake shoes had ground down to the metal, which explained all the noise I heard when I hit my brakes. Being somewhat new to working on cars, I had never changed my brakes before, and drum brakes had springs and clips that made them more difficult to replace.

Again as a poor student, I couldn't afford to pay for a brake job, but I could afford brake shoes, and I figured there was no better time than the present to learn how to change them! So, after putting my wheel back together, I drove downtown and purchased some new brake shoes, drove back to the school parking lot, jacked my car up again and proceeded to change my brakes. When I had the new brake shoes in place, a professor walked by, stopped, looked down, studied my brakes, and said, "You have the brake shoes in backwards!" I saw what he was talking about and immediately proceeded to reverse them! After changing the other brakes on the other wheel, I got in the car and carefully drove around the parking lot, testing the brakes. Everything was good! My first brake job was a success!

Later that day, I decided to drive downtown. After merging onto the highway, I was doing about 55 mph when the traffic started to slow, and I stepped on my brakes—THUD! They went right to the floor!! I had NO BRAKES!! With a sick feeling in the pit of my stomach,

I saw there were about twenty cars in front of me. The first car had stopped at a traffic light. I yanked the column shifter on my automatic transmission into low. That made a nasty racket but slowed me way down. There was a huge ditch on my right and lots of oncoming traffic on my left on the two-lane highway.

The first car's red brake lights flashed on, and then the red brake lights of the car behind it, and the red lights of the car behind that one lit up as well. All these red brake lights in front of me looked like a row of dominoes that had been tipped in my direction and were rushing at me fast! "Lord, what do I do?!?" To my right, I saw a small gravel driveway with bushes on each side, obscuring where it led. So, my options were to either smash into the car in front of me or flip my car over in the huge steep ditch on my right or hit an oncoming car on my left or try for that gravel drive.

I went for the drive—I made a sharp right turn with the backend of my car fishtailing throwing loose gravel and dust everywhere. Finally, I got the car under control and discovered I was heading straight for a mammoth carryout window with a bright yellow "Cold Beer" neon sign flashing in my face. That big old heavy car had a foot style emergency brake, and I stomped on that brake for all I was worth! The car went skidding forward in the gravel and slid to a stop six inches from the window! The people inside were staring at me, and I was staring right back at them, thinking, "Whew! Maybe I should check my shorts! That was close!! Thank you, Jesus!!!"

After taking a moment to recover, I got out and noticed brake fluid puddled on the ground by my right front tire but no brake fluid around the left front tire. I felt a little stupid as the people in the beer checkout line watched me as I jacked up the right front tire to work on my brakes. Getting down to the brakes, I saw they had smashed into a little metal unit with rubber covers on each end. Brake fluid was coming out of the unit and was everywhere. I didn't know what that unit was, but took it off and hitchhiked several miles back into town to the auto parts store.

Laying the messy thing on the counter, I told the parts, guy, I needed one of these for a '63 Mercury Comet. The parts guy glances at it and says, "Ok, you need a rebuild-it kit for a slave brake cylinder." At least now I knew the name of the unit. He brings me back a small box with a bunch of little parts in it and no instructions!! "Lord," I prayed to myself, "what do I do with these parts?" At that very moment, a guy walks up beside me at the counter and says, "I need a slave brake cylinder rebuild-it kit for a '64 Mercury Comet." My mouth dropped open. He looked at me staring at him and said, "Hi!" as the parts guy handed him a box identical to mine!

Since he was friendly, I explained my situation and lack of car knowledge. Right there at the counter, we opened up our boxes, and he showed me how to rebuild my brake cylinder with the parts and made some other useful suggestions about reinstalling the cylinder and bleeding the brakes. He then offered to drive me back to my car!

After the ordeal when I finally pulled back into my college parking lot as the sun settled beyond the Hudson River, I sat there in the purple twilight of evening amazed, thinking about my brakes and God's provision and grace keeping me safe . . . Once again.

"But let all those rejoice who put their trust in You; Let them ever shout for joy, because You defend them; Let those also who love Your name Be joyful in You. For You, O Lord, will bless the righteous; With favor You will surround him as with a shield."—Psalm 5:11,12 (NKJV)

~~ The End ~~

New Bride—New "Hamster"

\<\<\>\>

Married August 17, 1974, and then just one week later, we packed our wedding gifts and luggage into my old blue and white Ford van and headed north for Regina, Saskatchewan, Canada, where I was attending Canadian Bible College. When we reached the U.S./Canadian border, I pulled into the parking lot and took out my driver's license as my lovely new bride searched for hers. Back then, you only needed a picture ID to cross the Canadian border.

Looking at the roadmap as my new bride continued to search for her purse, I heard a GASP coming from the back of the van followed by, "Oh NO! I think I left my purse at home!" "Home" was Wheeling, West Virginia, on the other side of the country where her purse was most likely safely sitting....with her driver's license neatly tucked in a slot inside her wallet at the bottom of the purse!!

So, there we sat, a thousand miles away from her purse and ID and two hundred feet from the small border office on the North Dakota/ Canadian border. We didn't have the money to stay in a hotel to wait for the driver's license to be mailed to us. Plus, we were in a time crunch to get to the school, so my now distressed new bride and I joined hands and prayed, "Father, in the name of Jesus, can you somehow get Barby across the border without a photo ID?" As we were getting out of the van, I decided to take in a small photo album of our wedding to at least help prove we were married.

We went into the small office and approached the desk where the border guard was standing. After a brief greeting, I laid out my driver's license and then when my wife didn't lay out her driver's license, I sheepishly said, "Uh... we have a problem—we just discovered my wife left her ID way back on the other side of the U.S. in West Virginia. However, these are pictures from our wedding—we just got married!" I said with a proud grin. Opening the album, I showed him the basic wedding spread of photos, and soon we were joined by another guard and the secretary looking at the pictures with my new bride and me.

Showing them a picture of the pretty bridesmaids, I pointed out my cousin Jo, who, due to the rising humid summer heat in the small West Virginian church, fainted and knocked over the microphone stand on the way down.

It made such a loud BOOMMMMMMMMMMMMMMMMMM sound that bounced around the walls of the church; it caused some folks to cover their ears. To help, cousin Jeri rushes to Jo's side with the microphone still on beside her head. Jeri leans over Jo, who was now slowly coming to, and trying to make her feel better, Jeri quietly whispered as her voice was amplified and broadcast around the church, "IT'S OK, IT'S OK—NOBODY NOTICED A THING!" The border guards chuckled, realizing that everyone noticed everything, making it a wedding most would not soon forget!

Then I showed them a picture of me in the getaway van for our honeymoon sitting behind the wheel with a weird look on my face. My high school friends had jacked my van up and put it on blocks just off the ground, so my tires were spinning as I was going nowhere fast! We were all laughing about the stories as the guards chimed in with some of their own wedding stories. By that time, it seemed like we were all nearly family; they must have believed we were who we said we were and didn't need an official ID card to prove it as they wished us well in our new married life together while we walked out the border office door.

As we drove through the U.S. border onto the Canadian side, I looked over at my new bride who was sitting in the passenger seat smiling. "Wow! Praise the Lord!" He had answered our prayer, and down the road, we drove—making it in good time for us to get settled in our new apartment and start school!

Months later, at the end of the school year, my still new bride and I were now headed back to the States in the same old Ford van. Sitting in the Ontario line of traffic to cross through the Canadian border back into the United States, I was thinking about our move back to the States after having lived in Canada for a year when I noticed a border guard pointing his finger at me and then waving me over to where he was standing.

With a not-so-friendly look, he pointed at a row of ten garages and waving me forward, said flatly, "Park your van in garage number six." As I pulled into the garage, the large garage door rattled and fell shut behind us with a loud THUD. Looking worried at each other and feeling trapped, we weren't sure what was going on!

Two armed guards approached our van and politely but with authority asked us to step out of the van. It turned out we had been randomly selected to be searched before crossing back into the States. Since we didn't have any guns, bombs, or drugs in the van, this would normally not be a big deal, but what I **did** have buried in the middle of the van to keep out of sight was an undocumented pet ferret.

The ferret had been a wedding present from my best man, Norm; it was an albino, all white, pink-eyed ferret that we called Goofus, a fitting name since he seemed really goofy to us—but a lot of fun! One time with some friends, I put him high up on an empty fireplace mantel to see how he might try to get down. He wobbled along on his short stubby legs to one end and looked over the edge—"Nope!" He decided that was too far of a drop to the ground for him! Wobbling to the other end of the mantel, he looked over that edge and seemed to draw the same conclusion. Then, he did what I least expected—he turned around and started backing his little furry white rear-end over the side of the mantle. He must have figured if he couldn't see where he was going to hit the ground—he'd be okay. I caught him when he dropped, and we all had a good laugh.

Now, at the border crossing, Goofus was a problem because I didn't have any papers from the States to prove that he had been born and raised in captivity and that I had not taken him from the wild. This meant the border guards would likely seize and keep him. "Lord," I prayed, "I really like Goofus; can you please get us through this so that I can take Goofus back with us? In Jesus' name, Amen." The big tall, burly guard had me open the sliding door at the side of my van. The first thing he saw was my guitar case lying on top of the pile. "Please remove your guitar case, hold it at arm's length, and open it slowly." Feeling a bit intimidated, I followed his instructions exactly as given.

At the same time, the short border guard started rummaging through our stuff when I hear him loudly shout, "What's this??!!" He pulled up the cage from its hiding place to get a better view; hearing the shout, the big tall guard leaned into the van to see what his partner had found. Focused on the exposed cage, both guards saw our furry white Goofus staring back at them with his little beady pink eyes. The short guard said to the big guard, "What is it?" to which the big guard replied, "I think it's a hamster."

Now a hamster is usually about five-inches long from head to stubby tail, and a ferret is about twenty inches long and four times the size. Dumbfounded by their confusion the first thing that popped out of my mouth was, "Wow, you really know your animals!!" To that, the big guard grew a large, self-satisfied smile, and I smiled right back at him because I knew it was "OK" to take a hamster across the border!

As we crossed the border into New York, I was reflecting on our two border predicaments—both going in and coming out of Canada and prayed, "Father, thank you so much for rescuing us both times at the border—for getting my new bride across the border with no ID, and this time, for turning my ferret into a hamster! *(wink, wink)* A-men!!"

"If you then, imperfect as you are, know how to give good gifts to your children, how much more will your Father in Heaven give good things to those who ask Him!" —Matthew 7:11 (WNT)

~~ The End ~~

'Twas the Night Before Christmas—And No Presents

<<>>

Over the years my mother told me this story multiple times. Even after sixty plus years, that Christmas morning remained a vivid and special memory for my mother. During the Great Depression, my mother's family was very poor. My grandfather had a heart attack at age twenty-five; that left him in a weakened condition for years. And as the Great Depression settled in, there were few jobs for someone in his condition and those he did get . . . Paid little. They had four children at the time, and life was hard.

They trusted the Lord and survived on the generosity of family and friends, most of whom lived on farms, so during the summers Grandma would can a lot of produce for the winter months. Grandpa's brother had a good job and always supplied the family with milk. Beans were the main staple since meat was hard to get and very expensive.

A pot of beans was always on the stove, and my witty aunt jokingly said they ate so many beans that she understood why we are called, "human-beans!" Staying warm in the winter was not easy, but they lived near a railroad track not far from a rail yard. All the jerking of the cars as a train started rolling would cause loose coal to fly off the open coal cars. Grandma would send the kids to go collect what coal they could find on the tracks for heating their home.

The Christmas of my mother's memory had been an especially difficult year financially for the family. The kids had their church play and received their little bags of candy, each with its one chocolate drop—the only chocolate they'd have for the entire year, so it was very special. My mom was about six years old, and that Christmas had her little heart set on getting a stand-up dolly with real hair she could comb. However, she and her sister and brothers had no idea how bleak Christmas was going to be. Grandma and Grandpa felt terrible that Christmas Eve as they gathered together their children for bedtime prayers.

Grandma was always focused on the Lord and the practical things of life, so she never spoke too much about Santa and all that business. The kids huddled around their mother as she said, "This has been a difficult year. The Lord has provided, and we still have a home and food to eat. And for this, we are grateful! Your father and I have not been able to buy you the Christmas presents you would like for this Christmas. Truthfully it's worse . . . We haven't been able to buy you any presents this Christmas. So, let's try not to think about ourselves tomorrow morning on Christmas Day but remember the gift of the little baby Jesus that God has given to us. He gave us the Greatest Gift of all!"

With that, they said their prayers and climbed into bed. Grandma walked down the winding stairs gliding her hand along the old, worn wood banister as she descended, praying in her heart, "Oh Father, if there is some way, by some miracle you could give the kids presents for Christmas morning, I would be so grateful." And with tears, she stepped down into the living room to read her Bible for the night and pray for relatives and other struggling families.

SQUEAL, thump, BAM! Penetrated the house as metal hit the ground outside! A large truck had pulled up to the front of the house. Grandma and Grandpa heard it, the kids heard it, and then they heard the pounding at the door. On the dark porch, stood a smiling man holding a box.

Stunned, my grandparents watched as this stranger carried in the box and put it under their empty Christmas tree. Grandma saw the kids peering through the upstairs banister and told them to stay up there. Then the man brought in another box, and another, and more boxes, and then even more boxes!!

He was a local businessman who every Christmas would pick out some poor families and give them the toys he had left over from his Christmas sales. He brought in so many toys that Grandma filled a closet with them for future birthdays and the following Christmas! The kids were beside themselves with excitement, but Grandma made them go back to bed. She profusely thanked the man, and then in her heart said, "Thank you, Jesus, thank you, thank you so very much!"

Christmas morning came, and Grandma and Grandpa made the kids, wide-eyed with excitement, stand together around the gifts holding hands. Grandma prayed, "Thank you again, dear Jesus, for providing Christmas presents for our children, and may they always see your hand in their lives. In Jesus name, Amen!"

The kids dove into the pile with giggles and glee, and my mom climbed out with a long box. She opened the box, and her little heart nearly burst . . . Inside was a stand-up dolly with real hair she could comb.

"Delight yourself in the LORD, and he will give you the desires of your heart." —Psalms 37:4 (NIV)

"But seek first his kingdom and his righteousness, and all these things will be given to you as well." —Matthew 6:33 (NIV)

~~ The End ~~

Phil-Bill's Hungry Prayer

<<>>

Friends and family called him Phil; business associates called him Bill. He was a brilliant older gentleman, highly esteemed in the world of metallurgy. He had helped NASA with a rocket welding problem and made the final welds at the top of the famous Saint Louis Gateway Arch. I had the honor of being both his friend and business associate...so I called him Phil-Bill.

On long business trips together he shared stories with me about his life. He was a survivor of multiple car crashes and other tragedies. In every instance, he would always point out how God had protected him because, in the natural realm, he really should have been killed. One of his stories has stayed with me over the years—perhaps because it illustrates the simplicity of his faith.

As a young salesman getting established, Phil-Bill traveled a lot. Occasionally, he barely had enough money to get from one place to the next, hoping for a sale. Such was the case one lonely afternoon. He had only enough to pay for his stay at the hotel but not enough to buy food. He sat there on his bed, lonely, hungry and a bit despairing.

These were times long ago, and the hotel room had a rickety old bed, noisy springs, hardwood flooring, and a large vent above the door frame that slanted into the room. Turning to the Lord, Phil-Bill got on his knees beside the bed.

"Dear Father, in the name of Jesus, I thank you that I'm yours, but Father, I am out of money, and I'm really hungry. And ..." THUMP!

His prayer broke off at a loud thump right beside his head! He opened his eyes, and just a few inches away lay a brown paper bag.

Phil-Bill, leaning forward, opened the bag to find a sandwich with an apple. Dumbstruck, he stared at the food. Closing his eyes, and with a smile, he said, "Thank you, Father, for so quickly answering my prayer!"

I remember him telling me it was an excellent sandwich! Later, he found out what happened. Three gentlemen were standing near his door discussing their lunch plans. One had a bag lunch; the other two didn't. After deciding to go to a restaurant, the man with the lunch just tossed it up through the open vent above Phil-Bill's door.

Once again, God had taken care of him. He was always telling me that God was faithful, that He was reliable, and could be trusted completely. Phil-Bill lived that simple faith in his life, which was so clearly illustrated by his simple hungry prayer that was answered with a THUMP on his bed by his head.

"...for your Father knows exactly what you need even before you ask him!"
—Matthew 6:8 (NLT)

~~ The End ~~

Sold Our Home on the R-A-D-I-O

With my first real job after graduating from college, my wife and I purchased an old farmhouse in a low-income neighborhood—a great buy, or so I thought at the time. I figured it would go up in value...it never did. It was an original homestead in the area and was over a hundred years old with two floors and a huge attic that made it three stories tall. It had a very large yard with a century-worn old red barn in the back.

The first house on the street corner beside our driveway was painted a bright fluorescent green—so bright, in fact, it almost hurt your eyes to look at it. New to the neighborhood, I wanted to find out what kind of "nut" would paint their house that color. It seemed capable of glowing in the dark!

The sound of the doorbell brought my new neighbor into view. He was a tall and very elderly dignified looking gentleman with a cane and was wearing large dark sunglasses. Introducing himself as Ernest, he invited me in and in short order was telling me all kinds of stories about the area, especially about the great flood that hit Columbus, Ohio, way back in the year "nineteen-O-and-six." Later I learned the flood was actually in 1913, but at his age, being seven years off didn't mean much. Anyway, we quickly became friends. Then the question.

"Hey, Ernest, why is your house painted such a bright green color?"

"Wel-l-l," he drawled, "I'm legally blind, but I can still see some. As my eyes got worse, I started having trouble finding my house when I got off the bus. Then I got the green idea, and I haven't had a problem finding it since!" he said with a grin.

Soon after, I discovered that Ernest loved Jesus like myself, and during the five years we lived there; we had some good talks about the Lord. In fact, Ernest had such a passionate desire that others come to know his Savior too that he gave my three toddlers each a little green Gideon New Testament—he certainly had a thing about green!

His bright green garage bordered our driveway with just a few inches between the two; our drive went up a little hill, which put the drive on a diagonal about three feet high from the bottom of Ernest's garage. One day while working out in the backyard, I heard a loud "BOOM!" with a crunching metal sound following. Running around to the source of the sound, I saw this big old bronze-colored Buick half in our driveway, and half stuck into the side of Ernest's empty garage. The front end was suspended in midair, filling the emptiness of his garage. Bright green concrete blocks were laying everywhere.

Running over, I yanked open the door and shouted over the motor, "Are you okay??"

Reaching across the elderly woman, I turned off her car's engine.

With her voice quivering she said, "Yes, I'm fine—just a little rattled; I have a cast on my right foot, and when I went to hit the brake, my foot slipped off and hit the gas, and I guess my cast got stuck under the brake pedal!" And that's when she shot up our little driveway hill and through the side of Ernest's garage.

The squad came, checked her out and took her home. By this time, Ernest was standing by me beside his garage. Knowing he couldn't see, I said, "Hey, Ernest, you got a big ole hole in the side of your garage!"

Smiling, he said, "One of the good things about being blind is—the garage looks fine to me!"

When we bought the old farmhouse, we bought it on a land contract that ballooned in five years. That meant in five years we would have to pay the old German man who we bought the house from the balance we owed on it. Being young, that seemed far, far away; I had no idea how quickly time would pass and land us in a financial mess.

During those five years, sadly the cool old man passed away, and the house went to his wife. Soon after, she, too, passed away, and the house went to their two daughters. One was nice; one was nasty. There was such a fuss between the two sisters about our mortgage payment that we had to send two checks with half the amount to each sister separately—neither sister trusted the other to handle the money as a single account.

Reaching the end of our land contract after five years, the two sisters understandably wanted their money for the farmhouse. For many months prior, we had been trying to sell the house; however, there were two major strikes against the property. First, it was "atypical" of the area because nobody else had a barn, so the FHA (Federal Housing Administration) would not approve a loan on the house.

And second, it was considered a fixer-upper...being over a hundred years old; it still needed a lot of work. We even brought back the original realtor who sold it to us to help us try to sell the place again.

Those that were in the market for buying a house didn't want a fixer-upper that old, and those that were looking for affordable housing couldn't get an FHA loan because it was atypical.

We were stuck, and things looked mighty grim!

On Wednesday before the last week when the balance on the farmhouse was due, the nasty sister called and said, "If you don't get me my money by next week Friday at noon, I will sue you for all you've got!!" That's when I got out my big old rickety wooden ladder, climbed to the top of our three-story roof, laid hands on the house and prayed that the Lord would make-a-way for us to be able to sell our old farmhouse.

Saturday morning before that final painful week, my wife and I prayed, "Lord, we certainly don't want to be sued, but we don't know what to do. We need Your help!"

Sitting on the bed watching our twin daughters play with their baby brother in our large farmhouse bedroom on that summer Saturday afternoon, my wife had the radio tuned to a Christian station. A program called, "Trade-E-Ola," was airing at the time. Folks would sell or trade things like used vacuum cleaners, cookware, toys, bicycles, etc. My wife suddenly looks up at me as I walk into the room and says, "I wonder if they would accept a house for sale on Trade-E-Ola?"

She calls the show. "Lady, we've never sold a house over the radio before, but we'll give it a try!"

We prayed and waited, listening for my wife's recorded message about the house. She had called near the end of the show, so we weren't sure if it'd even make it on the air or not, but we prayed it would since the show broadcast only on Saturdays. As we saw it, this was our last hope. Then, like music to our ears, we heard her recorded message loud and clear on the good ole R-A-D-I-O! In reality, it seemed pretty crazy to us that we were resorting to trying to sell a house on an old pots and pans radio show, but we certainly were!

The weekend passed, and the clock started ticking down to Friday when the money was due in full.

On Monday a lady called; she was looking for a house with some storage area for her son's drywall business and had heard my wife's message on Trade-E-Ola about the house with a barn on the property.

Tuesday, nothing.

Wednesday morning the nasty sister calls again with a vivid reminder, "If you don't have my money or a buyer by 12 o'clock noon Friday, then you can plan on seeing me in court!!"

On Wednesday afternoon, the lady that called on Monday calls again and wants to look at the property. That evening she comes over.

Soon after opening up the conversation about the house, my wife finds herself saying to this complete stranger, "I believe in 'zaps' from the Lord, and we are trusting Him about the sale of the farmhouse." To my wife's complete surprise, the lady echoed, "I believe in 'zaps' from the Lord, too."

A nice chat continued briefly about the Lord and their families. Then, my wife explained the difficulty of getting a loan on the house, to which the lady replied, "I don't think that'll be a problem; when my husband died, he left me a large tract of land (in a wealthy section of town we found out later). I can use that for collateral with the bank if I decide to buy." (In actuality, her "collateral" was such that buying our property was like her buying a loaf of bread!)

Thursday, nothing. Friday's coming.

Friday arrives. This is it. We feel like it's our D-Day or rather Dread Day in our "Oh ye of little faith" moment. We didn't know what this Friday would bring. We had prayed and had done what we could. I was at work and continued to pray while waiting and doing my job.

At home, my wife went about her morning duties with our three small children...8 o'clock....9....10 o'clock. The clock seems to be in slow motion racing towards 12-noon, our deadline when the nasty sister was going to pounce on us. My wife remembers the deafening silence of that morning well.

Then, at 11 AM the silence was broken by the sound of the ringing phone. With anxiety and excitement, my wife says, "Hello" and doesn't remember much else except the words, "I'll buy your house." ZAP! God rescues us!

We call the nasty sister and tell her we have a buyer.

We give loud praises and thanks to the God of the Bible who heard our cry for deliverance, chuckling a bit that He could even use a Trade-E-Ola R-A-D-I-O show!

There was no mistaking it; LITERALLY, at the 11th hour, the Lord rescued us!

We would have preferred more of a time buffer, but it seems like it was our turn to experience the old saying, "God is rarely early, but never late."

And so it was.

"Wait for the LORD; be strong and take heart and wait for the LORD."
—-Psalms 27:14 (NIV)

PS: I recently found a similar quote and thought it was worth sharing. "God is never late and rarely early. He is always exactly right on time—His time." —Dillon Burroughs

~~ The End ~~

Attribution of Images:

Public domain Images were provided by the following websites:

MorgueFile.com

PixaBay.com

sxc.hu

—Bonus Stories—

<<>>

Not by Sight

Sitting there at her sewing machine, my wife gave me her attention as I came into the room saying, "Well, I've got our road trip mapped out; it should only take three months, through three countries, and around 15,000 miles." She stopped sewing, looked at me with her loving, caring eyes, and sweetly said loudly, "Are you crazy! You can't be serious, we have three little children!" But I WAS serious.

In 1987 my wife had quit her teaching job at a business university to stay home with our young children; I had quit my job as an environmental scientist with a state agency to strike out on my own as an environmental consultant, so for the time being, we were both jobless. Now, with time on my hands, I wanted to come up to speed on some current environmental issues, so my plan was to fly to an environmental conference in Tennessee and then fly to Washington,

D.C. to discuss some energy ideas with a friend who had helped design the COMSAT satellite system, and then fly home.

Another travel plan developed, however, when my wife said, "I'm not working, and you're not working, so why don't we drive the trip and turn it into a family vacation." So, sitting down with a map, I looked at driving from Columbus, Ohio, to Knoxville, Tennessee for the conference, and then realized we weren't far from Macon, Georgia, where I had some relatives, and that wasn't far from Sarasota, Florida, where some of our good friends lived, and that wasn't far from West Palm Beach on the other side of Florida where my wife had some relatives, and traveling up the East Coast, we had more friends and relatives right up to Boston.

And since I was on a roll at that point, the plan just kept rolling along from Boston to Chicago, down to Little Rock, Arkansas, to the bottom of Texas, down to Mexico City continuing to Guatemala City, up the West coast of Mexico, into Arizona, California, Oregon, Washington, up into British Columbia and across Canada, back into the States through Minnesota, Wisconsin, Illinois, Indiana, and finally........back to Columbus, Ohio!

That's why . . . when I presented my travel plans to my wife and at this point she clearly saw that she got a whole lot more than what she had originally bargained for, and so reacted with, "Are you crazy?" One good friend with great concern said, "Nick, I think you've gone off the deep end this time." My reaction was to go buy a twenty-year-old VW camper van!!

In the following weeks, we packed up the van with supplies for us and the kids and lots of spare parts and plenty of oil for the van. My son wasn't potty trained yet, so we had white disposable diapers stuck everywhere! Before leaving, a friend of ours gave us a little 3x3-inch plaque with a Scripture verse on it that read, "We walk by faith, not by sight." (2 Corinthians 5:7) We set the little plaque in a prominent place on our dashboard as it seemed the perfect motto for our trip.

The next day my wife, our five-year-old twin daughters, and two-year-old son climbed in the old van as I pulled the sliding side door shut. It was like boarding Noah's Ark only without the critters and the rain. Pulling left out of our middle-class suburban driveway, we worked our way to the interstate, and we were off!

I was enjoying the drive south out of flat Columbus, Ohio, the kids were playing in the back of the roomy camper van, my wife was sitting in the passenger seat reading her Bible and watching the rolling hills grow larger and greener with trees as we drove further south. The sky was a beautiful blue with wispy clouds, and all was serene as the old van purred along.

After passing through Kentucky into Tennessee, I noticed a lack of power as the van attempted to climb the hills. I chalked it up, however, to the van being a four cylinder that was loaded with family and supplies. But as we drove along, and as the hills got steeper, I became more concerned about the steady decline in engine power; then about half way up a very long high hill, it happened.

I felt the van jerk, and looking out the rear-view mirror, I saw a huge cloud of gray smoke coming out of the back of the van where the engine was located. I had flashbacks of a burning van I was in earlier in my life that caused me to have visions of flames and a possible explosion. I yelled to my wife to get in the back of the van with the kids and instructed her that when I slowed down, I wanted her and the kids to jump out the sliding side door. My intent was to get the van away from them in case it burst into flames or exploded.

In preparation for the exit, my wife pulled open the side door; then slowing way down, I yelled back to them, "JUMP!" Instantly, they all bailed out holding hands, tumbling into the tall grass by the road while I kept going till they were a safe distance away; then, I pulled the van to the side of the road, turned off the engine, yanked on the emergency brake, jumped out and ran back through the cloud of smoke to my family. We stood there and watched, but surprisingly, the big gray cloud drifted away, and nothing more seemed to be happening. Still, we waited.

After a good while, I walked back to the van, put my hand against the engine lid to see if something might still be smoldering on the inside, but the lid felt reasonably cool. Lifting the lid with great caution to inspect the engine, I feared that I might see all the wiring and parts burnt to a crisp like in my previous van, but to my complete surprise, they all looked fine, only covered with a layer of oil!

Checking the oil in the engine, there was not a drop on the dipstick, but since I had purchased plenty of oil before leaving Ohio, I was in good shape. After refilling the engine with oil, I cautiously tried to start the motor. To my surprise, it started! However, it was running very rough, like it was only running on three cylinders instead of four, and the smoke started blowing out of the exhaust pipe again. Going to the back of the van and putting my hand into the exhaust cloud, I felt it was oily smoke and not a fire-based smoke. Obviously, something had happened to one or more of the pistons, and oil was being blown out of the engine.

The van seemed drivable, so we all got back in, and slowly, very slowly, we continued climbing the long, high hill. Soon, we came to a filling station; we needed gas, and I needed to check the oil. While my wife and kids made a potty run, I started filling the tank with gas and noticed a small puddle of oil forming under the van and realized the engine problem was even more serious than I had originally thought. Praying, I said, "Lord, what do we do now? Is this the end of the trip? We really need your help! Thank you ... in the name of Jesus." As soon as I finished praying, my eyes were drawn to a white plastic audio cassette lying in the dirt in a nearby parking spot.

Letting go of the gas pump handle, I walked over and picked up the cassette. The side I picked up was blank, but when I turned it over, I saw that it was a music cassette by a Christian band I recognized. It was Petra's album, *Not of This World*, and again my eyes were drawn to the middle song called—"Not by Sight." I thought about the plaque from our friend that was sitting on our dashboard and was reminded that indeed we are to walk not by sight, but by faith! Right then and there, I decided that no matter how bad our situation "looked," we would go on in faith trusting the Lord.

Filling the van up with oil and with a full tank of gas, we headed back out to the road and continued coasting down hills, and climbing them at a snail's pace, all the time fogging the folks behind us with oil smoke. After about ten miles and a couple of stops to dump more oil in the van, the engine seemed to be getting more critical. It was starting to get dark as evening closed in, and I began to wonder what to do. In another mile or so, we saw a truck weigh station, and I decided to pull in. There were only a couple of guys working in the isolated station with no trucks around that needed weighing.

After going into the little building to inquire about a nearby auto repair shop, one of the guys said he had a friend that worked on VWs but more as a hobby rather than as a business, but he thought he might be able to help. He assured me that there were no auto repair shops nearby, and his friend was my best bet for getting the engine repaired. He called his mechanic friend, who suggested that we stay the night at a nearby state park, and then drive, if I could, to his place in the morning. He said he lived back in the woods, and we would never find his place in the dark. He gave us directions to the park and his place and planned on seeing me the next day at 9 a.m.

We limped our way to the park, paid for a camping site, parked the van and got ready for bed by setting up the beds in the van, but before drifting off to sleep, we prayed and thanked the Lord for a safe place to stay and for a plan to get the van fixed. Waking early the next morning and figuring this was probably going to take more than one day to fix, I got out the only "tent" we had which was a screen house, set it up, and moved the family, sleeping bags, food, water, and cooking stuff into the screen house.

My family looked like they were in a cage for all to see as folks walking by on the nearby trail looked rather strangely at them. In my wife's own words, she recounts, "I remember feeling very silly; everybody knows you use a tent with sides to go camping, not a see-through screen house! What kind of novice campers were we?? Obviously, we hadn't taken Camping 101 or if we took it, we must have royally failed it!!! The passers-by had no idea we had a camper van that was in the shop being repaired."

This was back before the days of affordable cell phones, so as I drove off, there was no way for me to stay in contact with my wife or to let the mechanic know I was coming. Leaving early to make sure I had plenty of time to get to the mechanic's house, I followed his map through the narrow, secluded wooded park roads. It seemed like I was about half way there when the van died—it just quit. It was 8 a.m.; I got out my tools and tried working on the engine, cleaning oil off the connections and such to try to get it started again. By 9 a.m. I was hot and thirsty and realized I had left all the water with my family, and there was no other water in sight.

Hunting around in the van, I found a quart of apple sauce; figuring that it had liquid in it, I drank the whole jar which did little to quench my thirst. Back out on the engine, I needed to get it started to get to the mechanic. About twenty minutes later, I stood up from the engine and felt something funny happening inside of me! All of a sudden, I felt as if I had just drank a very large glass of cool water!! I thought, "Wow!" It took about twenty minutes for my body to break down the fiber in the apple sauce to liquid, and I felt completely refreshed and no longer thirsty! Loudly I said, "Thank you, Jesus!!"

A few minutes after that, I saw a large tractor coming toward me—it was the mechanic! He said he figured I may have broken down on the way, so he came looking for me. He hooked up my van, towed it to his house, and drug it up a very steep hill to his large garage. Even in perfect running order, my van never would have made it up his hill. In short order, he found the problem—a hole had been blown through a piston head! That explained the loss of power and the large gray oil cloud that traveled with us.

Our answer-to-prayer-mechanic said it would take him a few days to get parts and rebuild the engine, so we'd needed to stay at the park till he was finished. He drove me back to the park where we lived in our screen house for all to see for three days. I got pretty good at changing my clothes in a sleeping bag though my wife and family chose to take the long walk to the shower house. We literally came to understand what it meant to "live in a glass house." More than a cliché, it became our awkward reality.

After the van was fixed, our friendly and extremely helpful Tennessee mechanic picked me up and took me back to his place, and I drove our new happy, healthy, purring-like-a-kitten van back to my family.

It was the start of a new day and the beginning of our three-month, three-country, three-kid, 15,100-mile trip. We loaded up the van, piled in, pulled the ark door shut, and we were off . . . with a new engine and a renewed faith.

<<>>

"For we walk by faith, not by sight." —2 Corinthians 5:7 (KJV)

<<>>

Postscript: Our trip covered all the places mentioned except we never made it to Guatemala because we were robbed on a subway train underneath Mexico City and banditos got my passport—but that's a story detailed in a later chapter.

[This story is dedicated to Karen and Denise DM. who met up with us in Boston during our long road trip. Karen also took the photo of our family aboard the USS Constitution at the top of the story. Thank you Karen and DD, you guys are awesome! —Nick]

<<>>

The previous bonus story was taken from the book below.

To see the book below and Nick's other books go to: AuthorNick.com[1]

<<>>

---

1. https://authornick.com/

Walking by
FAITH
not by
SIGHT
A Collection of True Stories
NICK NICHOLS

3 Angels 3 Encounters 3 Blessings

<<>>

The following three encounters by the following three men will never and can never be forgotten by them ...

ANGEL #1

Late at night, five blocks down the street, my great Uncle Paul realized he was in a heap of trouble!! Earlier in the morning, he had taken a taxi to the large, downtown convention center that was about ten blocks away. After the sessions and then a late-night dinner with another salesman, Uncle Paul had decided to walk off his dinner and think about the events of the day by walking back to his hotel instead of taking a cab.

When he was about halfway back, around block number five, he found creeping into his consciousness an awareness of being surrounded by gang graffiti taking on odd hues in the light of the street lamps. Gangs of young men sat together on the steps of some of the dilapidated tenant buildings and appeared to be just lookin' for trouble. Uncle Paul focused as best he could and kept walking, passing more gangs and trying not to make eye contact. Only three blocks to go. Now, a gang trailing behind him started yelling, "Hey old man! I need some money! Got any extra cash on you?" Laughter followed with increasingly ramped up jeering and taunting.

No police in sight, nowhere to run, heart pounding out of his chest, he wondered how a grown man could make such a stupid mistake to walk alone so late at night in a shady part of the city, but it was far too late to think about that now. Years before, he had seared into his kids' minds, "Never, ever walk alone at night; always stay in a group, especially in a big city," but here he was—not following his own wisdom. Being a victim of a mugging was imminent.

While bracing himself for the first blow, a colossal powerfully built man matches my uncle's stride and instead of landing a vicious attack, takes his arm and with some authority in his voice says, "Keep looking straight ahead and keep walking." The gang dropped back as if on cue, and his newly arrived personal escort walked him the last three blocks to the steps of his hotel, giving my uncle a little friendly push to start him up the steps. Uncle Paul turned to thank the man, but in that blink of an eye, there was no one to thank. His companion was gone! With a puzzled face, he looked up at the doorman at the top of the steps who had seen my uncle and his new friend. But with raised eyebrows, he looked just as puzzled and shrugged his shoulders while opening the door for another guest.

Years later when my uncle recounted this incident to me, I'll never forget the confidence in his voice and the look in his eye when he reflected, "The Lord sent an angel that night to protect me! I don't care if anyone believes me or not. I was there, and I know that I know that I know what I experienced." Then, as a side note while chuckling a bit half to himself and half to me, "With all the brawn and adrenaline pumping through the veins of those teenage gang members, God certainly knew what he was doing by sending a powerhouse angel dude as a body guard—an escort that was no match for those rough, tough smart-aleck kids—one escort not to be messed with!"

That walk back to my uncle's hotel produced an encounter never to be forgotten, remaining vivid in Uncle Paul to the end of his life.....and I've often wondered which angel came to escort Uncle Paul through those Pearly Gates . . . H-m-m....maybe, just maybe . . .

ANGEL #2

Back in the late1980s, a friend and I decided to attend an inventors' meeting where a Congressman would be speaking about new legislation promoting future innovation. It was held on a Thursday night at our local Center of Science and Industry, locally known as COSI, located in the heart of our downtown city.

My friend and I worked together in a laboratory, and I had recently finished a simple innovation that would (and did) save our laboratory tens of thousands of dollars over the following years and only cost $300 for me to build. My chemist friend, who was from Russia, held ten international patents. Recently, we had been kicking around another invention idea in the lab, so we were serious attendees.

After the informative session, we gathered for drinks and hors d'oeuvres with other inventors, venture capital guys looking for investments and some inventor hopefuls, including myself, for some chat time. Standing there with a cocktail sandwich in my hand waiting to talk to a venture capital guy, I was thinking about the fact that I had not told my friend that the Lord had put in my heart the desire for creating some food production innovations. I was recalling some of the ideas I had been throwing around in my head for the last several months when suddenly a strikingly Herculean-sized guy thumps me in the chest with his massive finger and says, "I hate you guys!!"

In that moment of unexpected somewhat aggressive confrontation, I didn't know if I should fight or run! His angry comment was so out of place for where we were. Then I realized he was a bit tipsy and being at least two heads taller than me, I didn't want to provoke him, so I let him talk. He repeated himself saying, "Yeah, I hate you guys! You're always trying to think up a new way to lower the detection limit of an atomic absorption spectrophotometer!" That got my attention because that's the instrument I worked with in the laboratory!

He continued, "Do you know who I am?" But without waiting for a response, he continued, "I am . . . (and he mumbled his name that I didn't catch); with my first invention I received 27 patents! All the fruit trees in Southern California are sprayed from my patents!" Still poking my chest, he shot back loudly, "Why don't you guys put your minds to good use and come up with new ways of food production or preservation?" Without another word, he walked off, and I found myself choked up because he spoke about the very things that the Lord had put in my heart to do! Could it be the Lord was using an obnoxious burly bully to make a point by poking me directly in my heart as he spoke?

As I was still mentally jarred from what had just happened, my friend came up to me and said, "I think these venture capital guys will be talking all night, and we have work tomorrow." Checking my watch, I saw it was 11 PM, so I nodded in agreement, and we headed out the front door of the now-closed COSI building. It was a clear, crisp autumn evening, and the well-lit sidewalk was empty except for this little black beggar guy standing by the street.

He looked pretty ragged like he had been living on the streets for a long time. As he started walking towards us, I began fishing around in my pocket for some money to give him. Coming up to me, he asked, "Do you think I can get a job in there?", referring to the COSI building behind me.

I pointed up at the glass front of the building to a second-floor office and advised, "If you go up there tomorrow during business hours, they can tell you if any jobs are available."

Deftly, he moved in closer and got his face just inches away from my face, and that's when I was completely awed by his brilliant, penetrating blue eyes! Sticking his finger in my face, he declared in a very clear and strong voice, "It's time to just Praise the LORD!" Instantly, I knew he was referring to the food innovations the Lord had put on my heart that the big guy kept thumping.

Before I had a chance to say anything, the little beggar stepped behind me, and I turned to question him, but he was gone! There were wall-to-wall closed buildings behind me for a long downtown block and the open street in front of me; there was nowhere he could have gone in those seconds where I wouldn't have been able to see him.

I looked at my friend and voiced, "Where did he go?", to which he replied with wide eyes and a puzzled look, "I have no idea" as he slowly shook his head.

My friend left, and I went to my car that was parked nearby. Closing the door behind me, rather than turning on the ignition to head home, I just sat there to reflect on what had just transpired. I was so astounded by the beggar's words, his stunning blue eyes and the realization that he was so much more than he appeared to be—I had no doubt the LORD had just sent an angel to deliver a message directly to me. A message that could not have been any more clear: It was an unquestionable affirmation that my cluster of food innovation ideas were not just some rambling thoughts, but were concepts the LORD had placed in my mind and heart—thoughts that I needed to pay attention to. He sent an angel to lock them in place in my heart, to let me know I needed to be creative in that direction.

As I pondered the significance of these events that had just happened, my car became a holy sanctuary in the presence of the LORD, and my heart became overcome with emotion; I could do nothing but gladly embrace the moment, weeping as my spirit aligned with His will. I was completely undone before the Master Inventor.

There is no way to describe in mere words the impact of that late-night God-orchestrated rendezvous; it remains incredibly vivid in my mind to this day. It's true I didn't completely understand then, but I can tell you that Holy Spirit-engineered God encounters are not easily forgotten—ever.

And to be honest, I still don't completely understand, especially given the fact that to date, I have not come up with any food innovations that would warrant an angelic visitation. However, like my Uncle Paul, I don't care if anyone believes me or not—I was there, and I know that I know that I know what I experienced. Over the years I have come to understand more clearly that God has his own timing regarding the details of our lives—details that make complete sense to Him, which, in turn, become opportunities for us to trust our unknown futures to Him ....with hearts that are only fixed on Him. In time, He will bring all things about and all will become clear.

I fully expect to see that blue-eyed "beggar" again—the next time on his home turf in heaven—and I'll greet him with a heartfelt and hardy

"Thank you!" for delivering his, "It's time to just Praise the LORD" message that has long stayed very close to my heart.

> "All things were created through Him, and apart from Him not one thing was created that has been created." John 1:3 (HCSB)

Our God is still in the design business, and I'm staying tuned, waiting for the next step.

ANGEL #3

Terry and I are friends, and we go way back; we are old guys now and "way back" means we were diaper buddies! So, you might say I know Terry pretty well. Not only do I believe his story, but I also have some insight into his life.

Still struggling with some old issues in his life, he was in deep turmoil and kept asking God why the bad things that happened to him in life happened. Wrestling with these things had also taken a toll on his body, both physically and emotionally.

Internally, things had gotten so bad he felt like his life had no value and no future; he was just barely existing day after long day.

Then one day while in his driveway cleaning out the back of his car, he pulls his head out of the back seat, standing up to give his back a rest, and he notices a woman standing on the sidewalk near his house.

Living in a nice suburb of Las Vegas, he knew his neighbors, and he knew he had never seen this woman before, so he assumed she was a relative or friend visiting one of his neighbors. Being the only other person outside on the warm, sunny day besides himself, he couldn't miss seeing her.

Appearing to be a nice-looking woman in her early 30s, she proceeded to walk to Terry who was still next to his car, and instead of the normal, "Hello" one might expect, she questioned, "Do you believe in Jesus?" Terry thought that was pretty odd but responded, "Yes!"

As she stepped in closer, Terry instantly felt peaceful and knew that everything that was happening was supposed to happen. Then she requested, "Can I pray for you?" Living and ministering in Las Vegas, Terry is very reluctant to have a total stranger pray for him because of previous encounters with bizarre and weird, cult-type people.

But surprisingly, because of how everything felt so right, he found himself saying, "Yes!"

She reached across with her right hand and took his right hand in hers and held it as she started to pray. Immediately, Terry felt like she knew him and knew his future. Even more profoundly, he no longer felt like his life was useless and of no value; in an instant, he now had a future filled with hope! He was overwhelmed by a sense of wellness and peace, which he hadn't felt for years.

He was also amazed at how soft her hand was; in fact, it was the softest hand he had ever held in his life. With Terry being an artsy guy and an accomplished musician, he is more aware than most about his surroundings and feelings and the contrast of things.

The truth is that he was quite distracted by how unearthly soft her hand was that he wasn't listening closely to her prayer, but he was aware that she was praying about his future. When she finished, Terry recounted that the smile she smiled at him was a beautiful smile that just didn't quit!

As she backed away, Terry voiced, "God bless you!"

As beautiful as her smile was the first time, he expressed that her smile the second time was completely indescribable—it was heavenly, a smile and face he will never forget. Ever!

She walked behind his car to leave, and Terry stuck his head back in his car to continue cleaning, mulling over what had just happened. In no more than a minute, he pulled his head out again, curious to see where she was walking to, but she was gone!

Terry lives on a straight street, and there is nowhere she could have gone out of his sight in that minute. He walked down his driveway to the sidewalk to look further down into the neighborhood, a very open area, but . . . no sight of her.

Walking back into his house, as he stepped into the kitchen, the first thing his wife Donna noticed was the peace that emanated from his face that she hadn't seen in years.

Terry started, "Donna, you'll never believe what just happened to me!"

Before she could even catch herself, the Holy Spirit flowed out of her, "You met an angel!"

And indeed, Terry had.

<<>>

The previous bonus story was taken from the book below.

To see the book below and Nick's other books go to: AuthorNick.com[1]

<<>>

---

1. https://authornick.com/

UNEXPECTED
GOD
ENCOUNTERS
A Collection of True Stories
NICK NICHOLS

The Thing Behind the Curtain

<<>>

Snowflakes drifted past the glowing streetlights, gently falling to the soft, fluffy white blanket of snow covering the frozen ground. It was a perfect evening for caroling. At ten years old, I could hardly wait for Christmas to arrive—not only the gifts but also our traditional Christmas caroling created even more anticipation of the holiday.

Every year a group of folks from our church would drive around the neighborhoods and sing carols to the elderly folks from our church who had a hard time getting out; it was a festive way to spread Christmas cheer, bring a smile to their faces and lift their spirits!

When our group arrived at a home, after piling out of the cars, my friends and I always managed a quick snowball fight before the singing started. At some homes, we were invited in while at other homes, we would try to read our caroling booklet under the dim porch light while the old folks would stand smiling by their open door, sometimes joining us in singing the old familiar tunes.

And often these old folks were ready for us! When the singing stopped, out came the cookies!! Instantly turning a chunky kid like me into all smiles! I loved the caroling and the cookies or maybe it was the other way around—the cookies and the caroling! But of all the old folks we went to sing to, there was one home I dreaded going to.

Old Mrs. Trimble's home scared the willies out of me! She lived in an older section of town where we climbed up the crumbling concrete steps from the street to her side of an old duplex. Every year, for the last two years in my short kid memory, she had invited us inside, and she never gave cookies.

The house smelled old, with old wood and paint, and it always had the weird mix of nursing home and ointment smells mixed in. But the worst part was the solid black curtain, behind which was—the Thing. As we entered, the Thing made groaning noises, short grunts, and screams, and you'd hear it banging around like an animal in a cage.

Everyone seemed to be ignoring this, like it was normal, but not me! I was terrified! Mrs. Trimble's living room was long, narrow and dimly lit; she would always sit in the back in a large chair, which caused all of us carolers to have to stand right beside the black curtain at the opposite end of the room by the front door. This time as we all crowded in, I was forced to the back of the group and right against the curtain next to "the Thing."

The caroling started and the Thing got more noisy and active—only the curtain stood between me and the Thing. I was always a very curious kid, and so, as scared as I was, my curiosity got the best of me, and I decided to gather up my courage and get a look at the Thing. When the moment was right while everyone was heartily singing, I slipped behind the black curtain.

At first, all I saw was the end of what looked like a big baby bed with its sides pulled up to keep the baby from falling out. Slowly walking around to the side of the bed, I stepped back shocked as the Thing came into full view—it shrieked, and I nearly wet my pants! But my curiosity kept me riveted in place.

The Thing had the twisted up body of a teenage girl!! Her legs and arms were twisted at unnatural pretzel-like angles, forcing her face down tight against the mattress, and she was looking right at me!!!! She made a low growling noise as foamy saliva drooled out of her mouth, puddling on the mattress. The wild look in her eyes was unnerving, and I stepped back further while the carols continued on the other side of the curtain.

I had never seen anything like this, and I was afraid at any moment she would leap out of the bed and attack me! Fascination and fear gripped me like a vice, but my eyes were locked on hers. Then to my complete amazement, in an odd sort of way, she smiled at me!

At that moment, I was no longer afraid, but completely confused as my ten-year-old little brain couldn't process this at all! As I quickly moved back out to the other side of the curtain, she made some more grunts and shrieks and for a moment, it seemed like she was calling for me to come back. Slipping back into the group of carolers as they finished their last song, we waved goodbye to old Mrs. Trimble and left.

I didn't tell anybody anything, not even my closest friends, except I did tell my cousin Jo who was like my sister about my moment with the Thing, or rather the girl, and what I had seen and experienced. It scared her too, because she had heard the Thing moaning and screaming during the caroling.

Over the years, as I grew older, I learned "the Thing" was old Mrs. Trimble's daughter who was born with multiple severe birth defects. She happened to be the younger sister of a lady I really respected in our church named Mary Ann and the Thing was the aunt to Mary Ann's sons, my friends Dan and Terry.

On the rare occasion when old Mrs. Trimble would come to church, she would sit in the back, and when the preacher said something that touched her heart, she would shout out, "Amen, Brother!! Preach it!!" And even more rarely, she would bring her daughter in a kind of large mobile bassinet, and would park her in the aisle where her daughter squealed and grunted through the service.

One of the things I really started to admire about old Mrs. Trimble was she didn't care anymore what people thought about her or her daughter! She had gotten past all that shallow surface junk. She just loved her Jesus and loved her daughter, and everyone knew it. She, along with her daughter, had actually become an inspiration to me to do what Jesus had put in my heart to do, and not worry about what people thought of me.

Now that I'm an old guy, I understand completely what was really going on when I met old Mrs. Trimble's deformed daughter. When I slipped behind that curtain as a kid, I had really stepped into a love story—the love of a mother for her daughter that was so great Mrs. Trimble refused to have her daughter institutionalized but made the decision to care for her as long as she was able. It was love upon love and total commitment.

I have since prayed that the Lord would give me the same love for my family as old Mrs. Trimble had for her daughter—the same unconditional love that Jesus has for us!

After I'm dead and gone, I fully expect to be strolling along the streets of gold in Heaven and be tapped on the shoulder—turning, I'll see a stunningly beautiful woman, whose eyes spark recognition that tugs at a long-ago memory. She steps back, and with a graceful flourish, stretches her arms out wide, and with a glowing smile says, "Do you remember me?"

"I was the twisted up 'Thing,' and look at me now!

Jesus, yes, my wonderful Lord Jesus...has made me whole."

<<>>

"He will wipe every tear from their eyes. There will be no more death or mourning or crying or pain, for the old order of things has passed away."
—Rev. 21:4 NIV

<<>>

The previous bonus story was taken from the book below.

To see the book below and Nick's other books go to: AuthorNick.com[1]

<<>>

---

1. https://authornick.com/

A COLLECTION OF TRUE STORIES
Spiritual
Lessons
THAT CHANGED MY LIFE
Nick Nichols

God Spoke, and I Looked in the Bushes!

<<>>

I will never forget The Voice. Climbing up the steep steps to my college library that cold December morning, my thoughts were on the paper I needed to do research for. The library was just opening, and I was alone on the steps. Suddenly my ears are jarred by this very loud and authoritative voice! "I want you to go to Canadian Bible College this coming semester and for the following year." It was so loud I thought my friends might be playing a joke on me, so I glanced behind the tall bushes by the steps. As I looked, my heart was telling me I had just heard God, the Creator of the Universe, verbally speak to me! Almost like Moses with some doubting at the burning bush I said, "But Lord . . . Nobody applies to go to another college in two weeks' time!!" He was silent, and I got the message.

It was two weeks before the end of the semester and Christmas break at my upstate New York college. The only thing I knew about Canadian Bible College was that my roommate had a brochure lying on his desk from them. I had never heard of the school before and didn't even know where it was located in Canada. The memory of The Voice compelled me onward, and I asked my roommate if I could have the brochure with its attached response card. I filled in my name, home address, and said, "Here goes Lord," and dropped it in the mail.

The school I discovered was located in Regina, Saskatchewan, Canada—1,500 miles from my home in Columbus, Ohio. This was back in the '70s when there was a severe energy shortage when cars were backed up for blocks trying to get gas. The airlines were having the same problem. Before leaving New York, I went to a travel agent to buy a round-trip ticket to Regina. I was told, because of the shortage, I could only purchase a one-way ticket to Regina, and I got the only seat they had left. So, in total faith, I purchased the ticket and went back home to Columbus for Christmas break.

At home waiting for me was the enrolment package from Canadian Bible College. I quickly completed the package and sent it to the school. As Christmas break drew to a close, I still hadn't heard anything from the new school. I looked at the ticket I had already purchased wondering if I had done the right thing. Here it was the day before I was to leave for Regina, so I prayed, "Ok Lord, you told me to go, and

I'm gonna go, but if I get stuck, it's up to you to get me unstuck!" Later that day, I received my one and only ever Western Union Telegram saying I had been accepted at Canadian Bible College for the coming semester!

The next day my cute girlfriend (later my wife Barb) drove me to the Pittsburgh, Pennsylvania, airport to fly to Regina. That was the closest airport I could fly out of because of the energy shortage. It was an unseasonably balmy 50 degrees for a day in January. Saying our tearful goodbyes, I boarded the plane still trusting the Lord.

The Regina airport back then had an old-fashioned design—the plane would land and stop on the runway, and then the passengers would disembark, walk across the runway and large open field to the mini-terminal. Shortly after crossing the northern U.S.-Canadian border, our plane landed; I stepped out of the plane and was stunned!

With the wind chill factor, it felt like it was 50 degrees BELOW ZERO! A 100-degree drop in temperature was a real shocker to my system! It was a very long distance to that terminal, and my parka was in my luggage; I was the only person running and yelling all the way to the terminal!

After I got my composure and folks around me stopped laughing, I dug out my parka and called a taxi. By the time the taxi came, it was dark outside. I shared my travel story with the taxi driver and the story of how I came to know Jesus. When we arrived at the school, she was crying a bit; I prayed with her and she only charged me half price. Now, there I was—standing in front of the small school. I walked in the front door and saw a light on my left coming from what seemed to be a micro bookstore. It was the day before the students were to arrive, all 200 of them, and an older lady was diligently organizing a pile of textbooks.

In my happy, cheerful voice, I loudly said, "Hi!" and the poor old gal nearly jumped over a chair! I, with long hair, a very large red beard, ragged hippie clothes, and sitting high on my shoulders tied to an aluminium frame was a giant brown canvas backpack—her reaction was understandable and, in the instant, she probably thought she was seeing Big Foot.

I announced to her, "The Lord told me to come here, so now that I'm here, what do I do?" After she recovered, she said she was in the process of closing the bookstore but would call the Dean of Men first and tell him I was here. She did that, turned off the lights, locked the door, said, "Goodbye," and giving me a wide berth made a hasty exit.

I was left standing in the darkened building with just the dim security lights lit. Out of nowhere I heard the tapping of footsteps, and in the dim light about thirty feet away, a girl stopped and stared at me. With the lighting and shadows, she almost looked like a ghost! As we stared at each other, she asked, "Are you Nicky from Columbus, Ohio!" I was shocked! This living apparition knew my name!!

It turned out she had been on a mission trip to Thailand the summer before with my girlfriend and recognized me from her pictures! On top of that, she said that she worked in Admissions, and when she saw my late application come in, she connected my name from my girlfriend's conversations, and so put my application at the head of the pile. Now, I knew how I got accepted so quickly into the school. While we were talking, the Dean of Men showed up, and he took me over to the men's dorm.

On the way, he said he couldn't figure out how I got accepted because every bed in the dorm was filled. He said, "For now, I'll just put you in one of the guy's rooms for the night, and when the rest of the students show up tomorrow, we'll try to find a place for you off campus."

While walking down the hall between the dorm rooms, this skinny Canadian guy comes up to the Dean of Men and says, "Dean, my roommate just left and said he wouldn't be back for this semester." The Dean looked at me, looked at the skinny guy, then said to me, "Meet your new roommate!" Clearly, "The Voice" of God had spoken to me as He went before me and "made a way, where there seemed to be no way."

<<>>

"And my God will supply all your needs according to His riches in glory in Christ Jesus."—Philippians 4:19 (NAS)

<<>>

Postscript: One other little thing. When I arrived at the college, I had ZERO money to pay for the semester. Since the Lord told me to go and had worked out everything else for me to be there, I figured He would take care of the money as well. When administration asked me how I wanted to pay for the semester, I smiled and chuckled saying, "Good question; I have no clue!" When they learned I had done maintenance work in the past, they put me on a maintenance crew. I shoveled a lot of snow that winter and did other things around the college, and at the end of the semester, I walked away with nothing owed. PTL!!!

Oh, and by-the-way, my new roommate and I became lifelong friends and are in frequent contact to this day—49 years later.

<<>>

The previous bonus story was taken from the book below.

To see the book below and Nick's other books go to: AuthorNick.com[1]

---

1. https://authornick.com/

<<>>

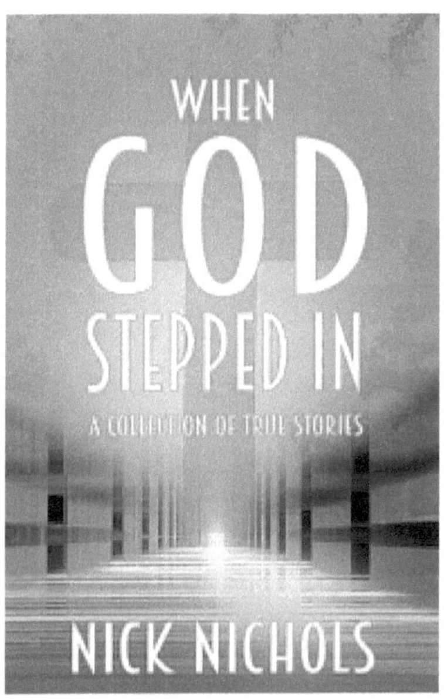

WHEN
GOD
STEPPED IN
A COLLECTION OF TRUE STORIES
NICK NICHOLS

Bankrupt . . . but Blessed!

<<>>

Laughing around our dinner table, my wife and I, and our four young children heard the knock at the door. Taking the stairs down to the front door in our split-level home and flipping on the porch light, I opened the door. There stood a tall man complete with a holstered gun, black nightstick, handcuffs attached to his belt, and a black jacket that said in bright yellow letters—SHERIFF.

Inviting him into the entryway, I said, "How can I help you?" But my heart sank; I knew why he was there.

"I'm here to serve you a subpoena; you need to appear in court, and the bank will be taking your home." I was stunned by his blunt statement, then immediately dropped my head shaking it back and forth. This visit was not totally unexpected, but hearing those harsh words certainly brought the reality of it out into the open.

Though he was just the messenger, in the humiliation of the moment, I found myself trying to explain how we had come to this point. After listening politely, he responded, "You seem like a nice guy, and I'm really sorry to have to serve you this subpoena." Thanking him for doing his job, I offered him some dinner, which he declined, and he was off into the night. Our dream home, the home we had prayed for, the home we had built, was now going back to the bank, and we would be out on the street, or so I felt.

Five years before, in 1987, everything looked bright, and my wife and I were a little fearful but optimistic as I struck out on my own as an Environmental Consultant. I believed this was the direction the Lord wanted me to take, and so I did. The average hourly wage at that time was about $9 an hour. The first year I charged $25 an hour and found work. The second year I charged $50 an hour, and no companies complained. The third year I charged $75 an hour and still no reaction. So, the fourth year, I charged $100 an hour.

One afternoon the CEO of a large national company took me out for lunch and said, "You know, Nick, you could have been charging us $100 an hour four years ago, and we would have happily paid it because we saw you as cheap insurance to stand between us and all the confusing regulatory requirements of the Environmental Protection Agency!"

As I began to realize my worth in the marketplace, I became more fixated on making money, and my relationship with the Lord began to drift into the background. Down in my heart of hearts, I knew I was off track and going downhill spiritually. Somewhere in there, I prayed in a meager mumble, "Lord help me to be focused on you and not on myself and my skills."

The answer to that prayer came with the recession of the early 1990s. In consulting, I was spending half my time helping companies unravel the complexities of federal environmental regulations and the other half of my time doing custom fabrication or repairs for non-commercial research laboratories and private industry. My standard practice was to put all the costs of a fabrication or repair job on a credit card. My billing cycle was every 30 days, so I could buy the materials, do the job, and pay off the card each month after the company paid me, and I would then keep the difference.

But as the recession set in, companies started pulling in their purse strings, and ALL my clients started paying me 60, 90, 120 days out or not at all! Some companies I had contracts with were very large, and they knew it would cost me more to go after my money than what they owed.

As the recession deepened, nobody was contracting the services I offered. This launched me into using credit cards for the essentials of living—buying food and paying utilities—and turned into the vicious cycle of using one credit card to pay another. Soon, I was in over my head, and in answer to my meager-mumbled prayer, it wasn't long before I was on my knees praying for help, and my focus turned back to the Lord.

As our debt increased, we began receiving calls from credit collection agencies. Every time they called, I would try to explain our situation and offer partial payment, but they would have none of it—"Pay the full amount, or we'll ruin your credit," they threatened. Some even started swearing at me on the phone and would call at all hours of the day and night, so I felt I had to resort to using an answering machine to screen the calls before answering.

Dealing with the creditor phone calls was certainly annoying, but it went to a whole new level when the neighbors started coming to me saying they had received a strange call asking if we still lived in our house, or if I still had my car and other such questions. The creditors were trying to see what assets I still had—and generally, harass me via my neighbors! And, yes, the creditors knew exactly what they were doing since everyone knows how embarrassing it is having your neighbors know you're sinking financially.

When I didn't think it could get any worse, it did . . . when I received notification in the mail that I was being sued by TWO companies! One of them was one of the largest and most prestigious law firms in our large city. I tried to negotiate with them, but again, no deal, and against my desire, they forced me into bankruptcy!! The last thing I ever wanted—but now, I had no choice. My wife and I were devastated, and we were so out of money that I couldn't even afford a bankruptcy attorney.

Needing to respond to the lawsuits, I went to our state Supreme Court law library and started digging into bankruptcy law. After days of digging, I discovered bankruptcy law was a massive pile of convoluted information with no clear direction—at least none that I could find.

One day standing between two large shelves of law books and in complete despair, in desperation I prayed, "Lord, I know this is all my fault from when I turned my focus from You to money, but I know you have forgiven me, and right now I need help and guidance about filing bankruptcy—I REALLY need help! In the name of Jesus, Amen." Still standing and despairing and staring at the floor, I noticed a skinny binder in line with the toe of my shoe.

Pulling out the small, thin binder, I flipped it open and almost fell over with shock—it was a continuing education course for attorneys who wanted to start practicing bankruptcy law!! It said, "#1. Tell your client to..., #2. Then file this for your client," and so on. It was a step-by-step guide of how attorneys should take their clients through bankruptcy! I bowed my head and said, "Thank you, Lord, for this awesome instant answer to prayer!! I know I don't deserve it but thank you so much!" I started following the guide and later found other useful legal self-help books.

As time went on, and as I kept studying and filing documents with the court, a date was eventually set for a court appearance. This had been a long and involved process; from the time the sheriff showed up at our door to this point had taken over two years—two years that we miraculously got to stay in our house! Before the court date, I filed a half-page brief with the court regarding a new bankruptcy ruling by the United States Supreme Court that I believed applied to my situation. The law firm suing me responded with a 32-page rebuttal!!

My day in court finally came, and it was intimidating. The courtroom was a large room with a very high ceiling; there were two old wooden podiums ten feet apart, one for me, and one for the opposing attorney. About thirty people sat behind us, and there was a large gulf of deep red carpet that dipped down several steps from us to the judge on the distant opposite side of the room and then back up a few steps to his bench. The judge sat in a throne-like wooden chair at a mammoth wooden bench that was surrounded by a very ornate wood railing. As I said, it was intimidating.

Looking beside me at the trim and fit law firm attorney in his $1,000 suit, I watched as he tamped and evened his handful of documents, ignoring me like I was a worthless piece of smelly street rubbish from the alley behind the courtroom. He was getting ready to go for the jugular—my jugular!! The judge looked at me and said, "Son, what is your stand on this bankruptcy issue?" I read my half-page document and then waited.

The judge then turned his attention to the confident, arrogant attorney who was just opening his mouth to speak, but before he could get a word out, the judge held up his hand for him to be silent and said, "Counselor, are you aware that the decision you based your entire argument on in this case was rescinded yesterday by the U.S. Supreme Court?"

The attorney looked stunned . . . and totally speechless. For a few moments, he looked like a deer caught in the headlights of an oncoming car. Trying to recover, he started rapidly tamping his wad of documents and then said, "But your honor, there are still the merits of the case to be considered!" The judge ignored him.

Looking back at me, the judge said, "Son, you have chosen one of the most highly contested issues in bankruptcy law; why, I don't even know what I think about it!"

Then with the crack of the gavel, the judge declared, "Case dismissed!" That was over thirty years ago. I was not sued; the bank did take our house, but with the Lord's help we were able to find a townhouse apartment that accepted a family of six.

Over time, the Lord restored everything to us including another house, but most important of all, the Lord restored my focus on Him!!

Yes, bankrupt . . . *but blessed!*

<<>>

"For the LORD will be your confidence and will keep your foot from being caught." —Proverbs 3:26 (KJV)

<<>>

The previous bonus story was taken from the book below.

To see the book below and Nick's other books go to: AuthorNick.com[1]

---

1. https://authornick.com/

< < > >

> < > : < > <

If you've read the sample stories from my spiritual books and want to have a relationship with Jesus, then here's how—

"If you want this light and love in your life, say a prayer like this—whether for the first time or to express again your passionate desire to follow Jesus:

Jesus, you are the light of the world. I want to follow you, passionately and wholeheartedly. But my sins have separated me from you. Thank you for your love for me. Thank you for paying the price for my sins, and I trust your finished work on the cross for my rescue.

I turn away from the thoughts and deeds that have separated me from you. Forgive me and awaken me to love you with all my heart, mind, soul, and strength. I believe God raised you from the dead, and I want that new life to flow through me each day and for eternity.

God, I give you my life. Now fill me with your Spirit so that my life will honor you and I can fulfill your purpose for me. Amen.

You can be assured that what Jesus said about those who choose to follow him is true: "If you embrace my message and believe in the One who sent me, you will never face condemnation, for in me, you have already passed from the realm of death into the realm of eternal life!" (John 5:24).

But there's more! Not only are you declared "not guilty" by God because of Jesus, you are also considered his most intimate friend (John 15:15). As you grow in your relationship with Jesus, continue to read the Bible, communicate with God through prayer, spend time with others who follow Jesus, and live out your faith daily and passionately. God bless you!"

Quote taken from the The Passion Translation

https://www.thepassiontranslation.com/

If you prayed the above prayer, I suggest you start reading the Gospel of John.

I prayed this type of prayer on February 2, 1971, and Jesus changed my life—forever!!

Blessings!

Nick Nichols

><>:<><

Professor Polly the Parrot

<<<>>>

Pulling me aside, the pet shop manager had an angry look on his face.

Poking his finger in my face he started in, "If that parrot says to a customer what you're teaching him to say—YOUR FIRED!" He punctuated that with a finger thump to my chest and a few choice curse words about me and the parrot!

That meant only one thing to me, I had to buy the expensive parrot and take it home for job security!

It all started simply enough when I got a job through my buddy Norm at a pet store while in high school in the early '70s. It was a crappy job, because that's what I was hired to do, clean the poop out of cages. Butt, being a critter fan, it wasn't all bad.

We had adorable puppies to play with, kittens, multiple kinds of birds, aquariums with colorful fish, lizards, snakes, hermit crabs, hamsters, mice, and occasionally exotic animals. Squirrel Monkeys were my favorite, we'd get around five of them in at a time and put them in a large cage. I'd put on a big long leather welding glove to feed them because as soon I put my hand in the cage, they would grab the food, bite my gloved hand, pee on me, poop on me, and scream at me! Eventually they calmed down, became less aggressive, and were fun to watch.

Another time we got a colorful bird called a Toucan that was popular at the time because of the Toucan that was on front of the Fruit Loops cereal box. That guy was beautiful till he ate, he would sling food everywhere. He was fun to watch eat . . . at a distance!

The fish we had were your basic Tetras, Guppies, and Gold Fish, etc, and once the manager ordered some Piranhas. Theodore Roosevelt in 1913 during his travels along the Amazon River in Brazil wrote in his best seller, "Through the Brazilian Wilderness," a great description about Piranhas...

"They are the most ferocious fish in the world. Even the most formidable fish, the sharks or the barracudas, usually attack things smaller than themselves. But the piranhas habitually attack things much larger than themselves. They will snap a finger off a hand incautiously trailed in the water; they mutilate swimmers—in every river town in Paraguay there are men who have been thus mutilated; they will rend and devour alive any wounded man or beast; for blood in the water excites them to madness. They will tear wounded wild fowl to pieces; and bite off the tails of big fish as they grow exhausted when fighting after being hooked." Later he witnessed a pack of Piranhas attacking and devouring an entire cow.

Those were the guys we had in our tank! Fortunately they were little guys about the size of a silver dollar. The big ones could get up to fourteen inches long, with a body about the size of my shoe. Anyway, one day a customer came in and wanted to buy a Piranha. Being the first time for me to deal with them I carefully netted the one he wanted and flipped him out of the net into my ready plastic bag of water.

Grabbing the top of the bag I gave it a quick twist trapping lots of air in the half full bag. After knotting the bag I was handing it to the customer when suddenly all the water poured out of the bag and the customer and I looked down seeing the Piranha flopping around on the floor. Grabbing my net I scooped him up and plopped him back in the tank were he went back to swimming like normal. Holding up the bag, we saw he had bitten a large chunk out of the side of the bag leaving a surgically cut scalloped hole!

After that, I was very, very, careful netting the Piranhas for customers. However, most of the time I didn't work out front with the customers, but worked in the back cleaning cages. That's were the problem started with the bird. We had a Red Fronted Amazon parrot covered with mostly vivid green feathers and a bright patch of red on it's forehead with some light blue feathers behind that.

She also had some yellow on her cheeks with some additional touches of red on her wings. She stood about a foot tall with a seventeen inch wing span, so she was a sizable parrot with a light colored beak and strong bite. Her previous owner had named her Polly, and Polly was an outstanding talker!

Being a parrot fan but never having owned one, I took a broom handle and stuck it between two wooden cage supports and would set Polly on it and talk to her while I was cleaning cages. She'd say things like, "Polly wants a cracker!" "Polly's a pretty bird." "Hey handsome!" "Hello!" "Bye, bye!" and other random phrases would occasionally pop out of her.

After a couple of weeks of this, and to vary her vocabulary, I thought it would be funny to teach her to say, "I'm a green son of a bi_ch!" I started working on her till the day the store manager walked in and heard me!!

After threatening me with being fired if Polly ever said that to a customer I asked the manager if I could buy the bird. He responded, "Fifty bucks and she's yours." At the time, that was two weeks of my pay! As I mentioned before it was an investment in job security so I bought her and took her home.

Polly got mixed reviews out of my parents who were willing to buy her a big cage which saved me another week's pay. The only place we found to put her that would keep her around us through the day, since she was a sociable bird, was in our kitchen by the window so she would see us and could look outside into our backyard.

My dad liked her right off, but she didn't like him! Like most parrots, Polly tended to be a one person bird. With all the time we'd spent together at the pet store, Polly and I had bonded. She would put her head down for me to scratch, but the moment my dad tried, she would threaten him with a screech and open-beak ready for attack!! It took awhile for her to warm up a bit to my mom, and for my mom to warm up to her too, eventually they got along OK but nothing like Polly and I.

As time went on, we would leave her door open and she would climb out on top of her cage and sit on a piece of wood we had up there. One of my dad's favorite things to do was when I would come into the kitchen, he'd run over to me and begin rapidly patting me on the shoulder and Polly, trying to protect me, would fly off her cage in a rage and dive bomb my dad trying to attack him.

Still with some agitation she would settle down on my shoulder and occasionally nip my ear because she was still railed up from my dad patting me. I belonged to her and she made that abundantly clear—and here I thought I owned her. Ha!

Eventually my dad did score some points with Polly. My dad loved Coca Cola and drank it every day and one time he was curious, and as I watched, he took a spoonful of Coca Cola over to Polly. She screeched at him as he inched forward with the spoon. With a sudden lunge she bit the spoon spilling the coke on the floor. My dad recoiled yanking the spoon back and she drew back into her fighting stance, only with a funny look on her face. She had inadvertently gotten a taste of Coca Cola.

My dad and I looked at each other, like, did she like it? He got another spoonful and inching closer she started screeching and screaming again, till he got within beak reach when she abruptly shut up and drank it! Then she leaned back, lifting one foot in the air while balanced on the other, she spread out one wing behind her raised foot while bobbing up and down making freaky chirping noises with her pupils dilating in and out from large to small! We took that as a, YES, she liked it!

From then on, the only way my dad could get close to her was with a spoon full of Coca Cola. Even then she would give him the evil eye, like that's close enough buddy! Forcing him to hold the spoon out at arms length. Then after downing her spoonful she would do her eye-dilating Coca Cola I-like-it dance!

After a while Polly got to the point of flying from her cage top to the kitchen table where my dad was sitting as soon as she would hear him crack open a cold coke. Which got to be annoying for my dad since she still wouldn't let him scratch her head without going for his finger. My dad started a no scratch—no coke policy, and that ended Polly's drinking days.

Speaking of my dad, he had to go to the hospital one time for some minor surgery and I drove over by myself to the hospital to visit him. After parking, I made my way to the first floor elevator to go up to his room on the sixth floor. On the second floor the hospital elevator doors opened and on stepped a pretty young nurse. She glanced at me and smiled; then she glanced at me a couple more times and her smile continued growing. Thinking to myself—"Hmm . . . is it my smile she likes? Or, maybe she likes my new cool woodsy outdoor jacket?"

I was getting ready to say something to her when the doors opened again and off she went . . . glancing back at me one more time grinning from ear to ear, and the doors shut. A few more floors up, I got off the elevator to go see my dad who'd just had recently come out of surgery. Walking into his room, and after greeting him with a quick, "Hi, Pop," he looks up at me and starts laughing. I'm thinking he must still be under the influence of the anesthesia.

Pointing at my cool jacket, he said, "What's that?"

Looking down, I saw I had this huge gob of creamy white and green parrot poop on my shoulder stretching halfway down the front of my jacket!! Obviously, it wasn't my smile or cool jacket that had the cute nurse grinning...thanks to Polly who had been sitting on my shoulder before I left for the hospital. Since Polly was a good-sized parrot, she'd dropped on me a good-sized load!

One thing Polly loved was to be set outside the kitchen in her cage to more clearly see the other birds instead of looking through the kitchen window plus she enjoyed the breeze. Coming in from our backyard garden one time my dad said, "Why don't we put her up in the tree and she can be with the other birds?" That sounded good to me so he threw a rope up into the tree and over a branch and fished the short end back to the ground tying it to the handle on top of her cage.

Pulling on the other end of the rope I hoisted her up into the tree and tied the end around the tree trunk. Polly was about twenty feet off the ground surrounded by leaves and birds. She seemed thrilled to be up there! One of the funny things while in the tree she often imitated the other birds she was hearing which left them really confused like something wasn't right with what they were seeing and hearing.

During the summer that became a regular thing, my dad or I would hoist Polly up in the tree where she would talk away or mimic the other birds, or loudly happy-screech! Frequently there were neighbor kids that would come around freely walking into our open backyard looking up in the tree watching and talking to Polly. The kids loved her, even the neighbors liked her and would put up with her occasional happy screeches.

One Saturday we heard a light tapping at our back door. Looking through the screen door I didn't see anybody because the bottom half of the door was a solid metal panel. Opening the door I nearly knocked over this petite, tiny, little girl! Looking up at me with great concern she shyly voiced, "Where's Polly?"

"Where's Polly? I repeated! I thought to myself, she's up in the tree, where else would Polly be. Walking out in the backyard I saw some other kids staring up in the tree, and looking up, there was Polly's cage door hanging open and no Polly!!

I told the kids, "Quick! Scatter and see if you can find Polly!" Running inside I told my parents and we each grabbed a handful of peanuts in the shell. Polly liked peanuts way more than crackers. My mom went out the front door turning left, my dad went right, and I ran across the street to look in the other neighbor's open backyards. We're all yelling her name, and we walked around for about an hour trying to find her.

Returning back to the street I saw a neighbor waving at me from about ten houses down. While running towards him he yelled, "We heard this screeching out in our backyard tree that was scaring my wife and saw a parrot up there, I figured it must be yours!" I trotted on down to his house and sure enough in his backyard tree sat Polly clearly enjoying her great adventure.

Coaxing her out of the tree with a peanut, I got her safely into my arms and to the joy of the neighborhood kids and the relief of our neighbor's wife I carried Polly back to her cage. Somehow Polly had figured out how to open her door, so from then on we added a heavy metal wire twist to keep it shut when she was outside.

Most summers, while I was out of school, we'd take a two week vacation to either see my aunt and uncle who lived in Titusville, Florida, or out to Denver, Colorado to see my mom's favorite uncle. This summer would be a Colorado run. Polly was good about us leaving as long as we left her with plenty of food and water.

I quickly loaded up her cage with extra food and water, rinsed my hands off in the sink, and said goodbye to Polly. Rushing out the front door I jumped in to our packed running car and we were off! I loved seeing my relatives in Florida, but my mom's uncle Paul in Colorado was something else! He could play a squeeze box (a concertina), the harmonica, and spoons he'd rhythmically slap against his leg.

To top that off, he was an amazing storyteller!! I remember thinking as a child, if I could ever tell stories half as well as my great uncle Paul, I'd be a happy camper! Well, maybe someday.

The two weeks of fun, music, and story telling flashed by all too quickly and we were back in our driveway at home, pooped from the long drive from Denver. My first thought was, how's Polly. My dad passed me his keys and I unlocked the front door and jogged in to see Polly. She was standing like usual on her thick wood dowel in the middle of her cage looking well and healthy.

She looked at me and instead of saying, "Polly wants a cracker," or some other phrase when she was excited to see me she only said, "BLOOP." That was followed by bloop...bloop...bloop, in a short staccato succession.

I voiced with a grin, "Polly want a cracker!?"

She responded, "Bloop."

"Polly's a pretty bird!"

"Bloop."

"Hello!"

"Bloop"

I tried the big one, "Polly want a Coca Cola!?"

"Bloop...bloop...bloop."

My mom came in followed by my dad to also see how Polly was doing.

I offered, "Polly looks like she made it through the two weeks okay, but..."

"Bloop...bloop...bloop," rolled out of Polly.

My mom started laughing because it was a funny sound that we'd never heard her make before.

"Bloop...bloop."

My mom thought she heard something. Being a former traveling and record cutting singer in a Gospel trio, she had excellent hearing, so she told us to be quiet and stared at the floor, concentrating on listening.

She reacted, "Oh, my goodness!"

Walking over to the sink she heard the soft sound of bloop...bloop...bloop.

Looking up, she started laughing again stating, "Poor Polly!! She's been listening to the sink faucet dripping day and night for two weeks!! She's imitating the drip sound!"

Apparently in my rush to leave on vacation, I didn't get the sink faucet completely turned off! It took me a week of talking and playing with Polly to get her to say her old familiar phrases again. Still, years later, once in a while, out would pop a, "Bloop, bloop."

At this point, we'd had Polly for over twenty-five years! Red Fronted Amazons were known to live up to eighty years. I didn't know how old Polly was when I bought her, but whatever her age, add a quarter of a century and she was probably getting pretty old.

I say this because she was starting to get cranky! And since my dad had also been growing older he was starting to get a bit cranky too. But mainly at Polly who he had shared his beloved kitchen with for twenty-five years and now neither were being nice to the other.

It was obvious it was time for Polly to move to a new home. I was in a living situation where I couldn't take Polly. I asked a bunch of friends but they couldn't take her either, so sadly I put her up for sale describing her as a good talker. Within a couple of days I heard from a guy who raised parrots and he had been looking for a parrot that could talk and teach his young parrots to talk. I assured him she could talk up a storm and would make a great teacher!

Not long after, he came to pick her up. It made me feel better with him taking Polly as I watched his interaction with her. He was clearly a parrot guy! My mom and dad and I stood on the front porch watching as he and Polly backed out of our driveway.

In a way, it felt like Polly was graduating as we waved our final farewells to now—Professor Polly.

>> The End <<

<<>>

The previous bonus story was taken from the book below.

To see the book below and Nick's other books go to: AuthorNick.com[1]

<<>>

---

1. https://authornick.com/

Critter
Tales
Adventures With
My Pet Pals
Nick Nichols

—Book Samples—

<<>>

Adventures of a Mall Santa

<<>>

Bursting into the photo lab David, the mall manager, said to me, "QUICK, put down what you're doing; our mall Santa cancelled, and we need a Santa NOW!!" On our way out the door he said, "I need you to be Santa for this week through Christmas Eve," and then almost as a second thought, he asked, "Have you ever been a Santa before?" I said, "No, and why ME??"

"You're big, you don't need pillows, you laugh a lot, and your eyes even kind of twinkle a bit," he said. I was dumb struck—thinking about myself as Santa!? The whole idea was so crazy and sudden that I burst out laughing with a "HO! HO! HO!!" to fit the moment —"SEE," he said, "That's what I mean; you'll make a GREAT Santa!!"

I thought about how getting roped into being Santa was an interesting twist from my regular life as a career chemist, a position I was giving up as my family and I were switching direction to head to Bangladesh to do economic development work through a mission organization. While we waited for all the details to fall into place, I decided this short-term job as a photo lab technician would fill the bill, not knowing that turning into an "instant" Santa was going to be part of the job description! However, in the excitement of the moment, I thought, "Sure, why not; how hard could it be?" As quickly as David had pulled me into this, just as quickly I decided I was up for the adventure! "Bring it on; where are my candy canes?"

David pushed me into a little changing room where several women helped me get into the Santa suit while another put on my beard and little glasses, another my hat and some rouge on my cheeks to give me the classic cherry-red cheeks that are a must for every Santa! There was a mirror hanging on the door, and I marveled at how quickly they transformed me from a lab tech into Santa Claus. I was so impressed I was half expecting Rudolph with his shiny red nose to show up at any moment with my sled!

Leaving the dressing room, we rushed to Santa's big fake-snow covered large sitting chair that had a huge picture of the North Pole for a backdrop and a little white picket fence surrounding the area covered with more fake-snow, glittering tinsel, and brightly colored Christmas presents that dotted the Styrofoam snow drifts inside the fence. All was lit up with colored Christmas lights and soft holiday music was playing in the background. Yep, the North Pole had descended to this Midwestern mall!

Lines were starting to form, and I had two hours to be Santa! Looking at the excitement on the little faces reminded me of how excited my children were when they went to see the mall Santa. All that got me smiling and waving at the kids and winking at a few moms, too, in good merriment! Yes, I could be Santa for two hours; I'd seen a million Santas in my lifetime, and I knew the game plan . . .

So with a little excitement mixed with a little fear and a little bewilderment from having never actually done this before, I saw there was no time for thinking about it anymore as a mother with her son in tow was heading right for me—"SANTA... you're on!"

[Story continues in book.]

<<>>

The previous bonus story was taken from the book below.

To see the book below and Nick's other books go to: AuthorNick.com[1]

<<>>

---

1. **https://authornick.com/**

ADVENTURES
OF A
Mall
Santa
NICK NICHOLS

The Mystery of Grandpa's Christmas Cane

<<>>

Little Christian started climbing up into his Grandpa's lap, causing Grandpa to yank the big family Bible he had been reading out of the way. Sitting it on the stand by his walking cane, he and Christian jostled around in his big easy chair till they were both comfortable. Christian was ready to talk, and his Grandpa was always ready to listen.

"Grandpa?"

"Yes?"

"Why do you use a cane?"

<<>>

<<>>

Leaning back a bit, Grandpa said, "Well, as a young man I broke my foot in an accident, and it never healed quite right." Closing his eyes picturing the events, he said . . .

"My team of five climbers and I were halfway up Mount Everest, the highest mountain in the world, when a storm started blowing in. The sky had suddenly changed from a brilliant blue to a stormy gray. As the wind blew harder, the temperature dropped, and we found ourselves trapped by the storm on the side of the mountain.

"Yelling to my team through the howling wind, I told them we have to turn back and go back down the mountain. That's when my foot caught between two rocks, and at the same moment, the climber below me slipped on some loose ice on the side of the mountain, and . . ."

"Grandpa!"

"Once he fell, his safety rope jerked my entire body, breaking my trapped foot . . ."

"G-R-A-N-D-P-A!!"

Opening his eyes, Grandpa said, "What!?"

With a serious look, Christian said, "Tell me the truth, Grandpa!"

"Ok, a cow accidently stomped on my foot and broke it. Back on our farm when I was a few years older than you, one day when I was doing my chores, I was trying to get old Jughead into the stall to milk her, but something startled her real bad—she jumped back and smashed my foot. And it's just gotten worse over the years."

Christian beamed with delight catching Grandpa in one of his tall tales. Grandpa laughed and tosseled Christian's hair, thinking what a sharp little guy he was. He was always so full of questions, but the older Christian got, the harder it was for Grandpa to get Christian to believe his "creative" answers.

[Story continues in book.]

<<>>

The previous bonus story was taken from the book below.

**To see the book below and Nick's other books go to:
AuthorNick.com[1]**

<<>>

---

1. https://authornick.com/

<<>>

Note: Photo attributions are listed in each book.

Don't miss out!

Visit the website below and you can sign up to receive emails whenever Nick Nichols publishes a new book. There's no charge and no obligation.

https://books2read.com/r/B-A-NVTG-XTXVB

BOOKS 2 READ

Connecting independent readers to independent writers.

About the Author

During my 30-year career, I was a water quality chemist, environmental scientist, consultant, and technical writer. In my spare time, I worked on projects in aquaculture, hydroponics, aquaponics, bioremediation, and renewable energy. In addition, I have also been an adjunct instructor at two colleges teaching Cellular Biology and Business Math.

Now I am retired and writing this from an island in South East Asia where I live. My lovely wife has been with me for forty-eight years and we have four awesome adult children and three lovely children in Heaven.

--Nick Nichols

<<>>

Read more at https://authornick.com/.